*Motorbooks International*
# POWERPRO SERIES
# HOW TO BUILD & MODIFY
# INTAKE & EXHAUST SYSTEMS

Ben Watson

First published in 1994 by Motorbooks International Publishers & Wholesalers, PO Box 2, 729 Prospect Avenue, Osceola, WI 54020 USA

© Ben Watson , 1994

Library of Congress Cataloging-in-Publication Data

Watson, Ben
     How to build & modify intake & exhaust systems/ Ben Watson.
         p.   cm. -- (Motorbooks International powerpro series)
         Includes index.
         ISBN 0-87938-947-8
     1. Audomobiles--Motors--Carburetors--Design and construction.
     2. Automobiles--Motors--Exhaust systems--Design and construction.
     3. Automobiles--Motors--Modification. I. Title. II. Title:  How to build and modify intake & exhaust systems.  III. Series.
     TL212. W38   1994
     629. 25 ' 33 ' 0288--dc20     94-33835

**On the front cover:** An Edelbrock Performer RPM intake manifold and an Edelbrock performance muffler, courtesy Edelbrock Corporation and Jim Losee; and a Holley carburetor. *Craig Lassig*

Printed and bound in United States of America

# Contents

# Introduction

As a teenager, I lived in London, England. During the 1960s this was a terrible place for an American motorhead to be. While my contemporaries in the land of burgers and shakes were cruising Doheney in their 409-powered '55s, I was trying to tell myself that riding a "Green Line" bus to get around was cool. Then there were all these "blokes"—that's what we called the young English guys—who thought the ultimate performance car was a Mini Cooper. While I grant you the performance of this car was amazing for 1275 cubic centimeters (a mere 77.81 cubic inches), it could not compare to a 426 hemi in anything. In fact, many of the blokes felt that school, music, and clothing were more important than cars. No wonder the British Empire has disintegrated. Sadly, I had to become a spectator and fan of Formula racing and "mud-plugging."

When I first ventured into the world of race cars myself, several years after returning to the land of drag racing and the Indy 500, I was firmly convinced that all a racing engine really needed was high-compression pistons and good, rich drinks of fuel. My philosophy was that since it was the fuel that exploded, it was the fuel that the engine needed most. The first incarnation of our racing engine featured a stock 2-barrel carburetor and stock 2-barrel manifold. The first evolutionary step placed a 4-barrel carburetor on the stock 2-barrel manifold. As we all knew in those days, the bigger the carburetor, the greater the power. We used the biggest Holley carburetor I could pull out of the scrap bin at work. The adapter for the carburetor was the only professionally constructed component in the entire intake system. For some reason, the engine speed used to max out at about 3800rpm.

The first race car I ever worked on was when I was in trade school in Glendale, Arizona. This highly professional venture featured a 283 Chevy engine with a "natural" exhaust system. I suppose I felt the best exhaust system was no exhaust system past the cylinder head. The rest of this car was as professionally built as were the engine and exhaust system. As a result, on its first trip to Manzinita Speedway, the right front wheel came off as the car entered turn four for the first time. After performing a near pirouette at the retaining wall, the driver and owner came to me and explained their frustration using practically every common word not in the dictionary.

Time goes on, knowledge expands, lessons are learned. I often relate these types of stories in technical training classes I teach around the United States and other points in the northern hemisphere. I related some of these stories in a class I taught in Vancouver, British Columbia, a few years ago. One of the students raised his hand and said, "Gee, you must have been a lousy mechanic..."

# Chapter 1
# Theory of Induction

## The Hundred-Mile Column

Above the Earth is a column of air that rises over 100 miles. Those who know about the world, the purpose of the universe, and the meaning of life, know that this column of air was placed here by higher powers for one reason only—to power automobiles.

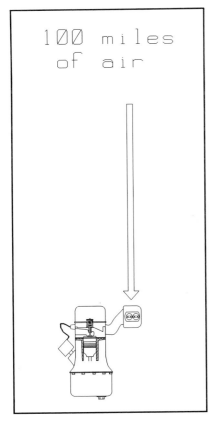

If you are looking around the solar system for a place to call home, and if you are an automotive enthusiast be sure to look closely at my home planet, earth. Unique in the solar system, only earth has a column of oxygen laden atmosphere rising over 100 miles above every point on the planet. Only earth offers a fossil fueled vehicle whith all the readily available oxidizers it could desire.

If one were to approach the Earth from space one would find that as he descended through the atmosphere it would exert an ever increasing pressure on his spacecraft. By the time our space traveler were to land on the surface near Galveston, Texas, he would find that pressure to be nearly 15 pounds per square inch (psi). The sole purpose of this pressure is to force air into the intake system of fire breathing internal combustion engines.

Contrary to popular belief, the internal combustion gasoline engine does not draw air into its bowels when it runs. Instead the piston descending in the cylinder stretches the molecules in that cylinder apart. As the molecules are stretched apart their pressure decreases. As the pressure in the cylinder drops below the pressure exerted by the 100 mile (mi) column of air, the air in that column begins to flow into the cylinder. The more the pressure in the cylinder is decreased, the more easily the 100mi column pushes air into the cylinder.

If the engine in question were to rise in the column of air, say for instance drive to the top of Pikes Peak, the pressure forcing its way into the engine would be lower. The cylinders would not contain as much air when the intake valve closes, the pressure in the combustion chamber would not rise as high as in Galveston, the pressure after ignition would not be as high, and less power would be produced.

Power comes from air. The earliest sailors of the sea knew this, every performance engine builder knows this, yet many people think that power comes from increasing the amount of

Any sophisticated alien race would realize the only reasonable purpose for having a planetary atmosphere 100 miles thick is to provide adequate pressure over the top of the engine to fill the cylinder of that engine to 14.7psi. Cylinders filled to this pressure can make good horsepower, cylinders that do not fill to this pressure cannot. Air is not drawn into the cylinders, it is pushed into the cylinders.

fuel. Increasing the amount fuel to increase the amount of power is effective only to the extent that the extra fuel can add extra heat to the air, to cause the air to expand. Add extra air and you add extra power. This book is the story of how to get extra air into the engine. The internal combustion spark ignition engine works as a unit to pull in air. The compression ratio is a factor in how much the pressure is reduced when the piston moves down. The design of the ports in the cylinder head can affect how much air can flow into the engine. The specific area that this book will address is how to make the maximum amount of air possible available to the cylinder heads and how that air, once

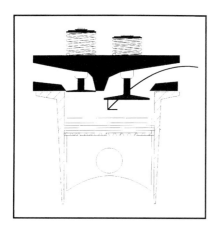

As the piston drops it stretches the molecules apart. This creates a low pressure area. The 100 mile tall column of air forces air into the cylinder.

burned, will exit the cylinder head. This book is about the intake and exhaust systems.

## Air temperature

Air temperature has a large effect on the amount of air entering the engine. Although the temperature will not have an effect on the volume of air entering the engine, it will have an effect on the number of molecules contained in a given volume of air. As the temperature of the air rises, the density of the air decreases. As the temperature of the air decreases, the density of the air increases.

Have you ever wondered why the little land rocket of your teens seemed to run a little better once the sun went down? Was this because of the excitement of a teenage night? After the sun goes down the air cools, becomes denser, so every cubic foot of air entering the engine contains more molecules. The more molecules of air there are entering the engine, the more potential power there is to be created from that engine. This means that an engine in Fairbanks in the middle of winter will be gulping a greater air mass per engine cycle than the same engine in Phoenix during the summer.

Many fuel injected engines use a mass sensor to measure the total mass of air entering the engine. At sea level pressure (29.92 inches of mercury) and at 32 degrees Fahrenheit (F), 1293 grams of air occupies one cubic meter. This means that every cubic foot of air available to enter the engine has a mass of about 1.29 ounces. If the engine is drawing 600 cubic feet per minute (cfm), the mass of air entering the engine is 774 ounces per minute.

As the temperature increases, the air becomes even less dense. At 100 degrees Fahrenheit at sea level, the density will be less than at 32 degrees. To calculate this effect, we need to convert our temperature readings into degrees Rankine (R). Rankine is temperature measured above absolute zero. Since 0 degrees (F) is 460 degrees (R), 32 degrees F is 492 degrees R, and 100 degrees F is 560 degrees R. Density decreases inversely with the temperature, so if there are 1.29 ounces of air per cubic foot at 492 degrees R, therefore at 560 R there will be 492 divided by 560 times 1.29 ounces, or 1.13 ounces per cubic foot.

When the temperature has risen from 32 to 100 the mass in a cubic foot of air has decreased from 1.29 ounces to 1.13 ounces. This means that the engine running at a speed where it draws 600cfm will now only be gulping 680 ounces of air per minute instead of 774 ounces. This means a corresponding potential horsepower loss of 12.1 percent. A well designed intake manifold will minimize this power loss by reducing the pressure drop as much as possible as the air flows through the manifold.

## Air Pressure

When most people hear the topic of air density discussed they confuse it with pressure. In reality, pressure is one of the things that affects the density of a gas like air, but it is not the only thing. Air pressure at the ocean surface of planet Earth is 14.7psi, 29.92 inches (in) of mercury, or 101.3 kilopascals. At the bottom of the Dead Sea the pressure is about 15.28psi. This is an increase in pressure of about 3.9 percent. This means that the force trying to move the air into the combustion chamber is great-

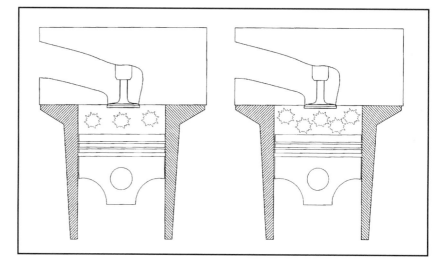

The more air that enters the engine, the more power there is that can be created. When the air is cold the molecules are jammed closely together, the closeness of the molecules means that more oxygen and nitrogen molecules provides extra power when the engine is started.

The mass air flow sensor is used on applications such as the Corvette 5.7 liter engine to measure the volume and weight of the air entering the engine. In the performance engine business a lot of attention is given to cfm, a volume measurement. Cfm is important, but what is more important is how much oxygen and expandable gas (nitrogen) is in the volume of air entering the engine? What is the mass of the air?

er near the surface of the Dead Sea (1,310 feet below sea level) than it is at average mean sea level for the rest of the planet.

According to *The Automotive Handbook* published by Robert Bosch Corporation, it is generally accepted in automotive engineering circles that increasing the altitude by 328 foot (ft) will cause a power loss of 1 percent. In like fashion, decreasing the altitude should cause a power increase of 1 percent. If an engine produces 300 horsepower at sea level it will produce 297 horsepower 328 feet above sea level and 303 horsepower 328 feet above sea level. This, of course assumes that the climate and weather do not change as the altitude change takes place.

This problem of power loss with altitude change is nowhere more apparent than at the famous Pikes Peak Hill climb. The race begins at about 6,000 feet above sea level near Colorado Springs. The race ends at the top of the mountain about 8000 feet higher. Now let us follow Bobby Unser to the top of

Pikes Peak. As he climbs the hill he and his engine will pass through about 24 of the 328 foot intervals. At the starting line his engine, already handicapped by being 6000 feet above sea level, will be creating the greatest amount of power that it will create during the entire race. For the sake of discussion let us say that his engine is creating 400 horsepower at the starting line. At 6328 feet the power of the engine will be reduced to 396 horsepower. When Mr. Unser and his car rises another 328 feet to 6656 feet the power will be reduced by 1 percent of 396 down to 392.04 horsepower. Note that the effect of the altitude increase has decreased a bit. This is because the altitude increase is meting out its affect on a smaller horsepower. The next 328 feet, to 6984 feet, will cause the power to drop by only

3.92 horsepower to 388.1196 horsepower. Notice in the following chart how the ever-increasing altitude creates a power loss while the amount of that power decreases since there is less power to lose at every interval.

As you can see, the engine loses nearly 90 horsepower during the climb. There are other variables that are not mentioned here. For instance, the temperature of the air at 14,110 feet is very likely colder than the temperature at 6000 feet. If the temperature of the air did not drop as the altitude rises this 90 horsepower loss would be inevitable. The air will be colder, therefore denser than if the temperature of the air was the same on the starting line and the finish line, this will, therefore, offset somewhat the lower atmospheric pressure.

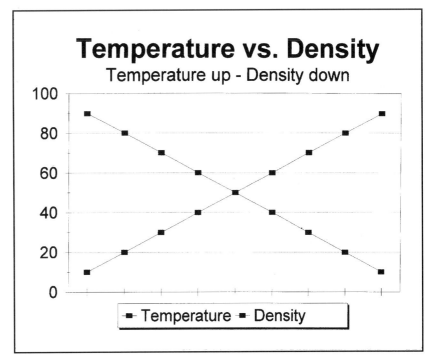

Air density is primarily a function of its temperature. As the temperature of the air increases, the density of the air decreases. This means that an engine in Fairbanks in the middle of winter will be gulping a greater air mass per engine cycle than the same engine in Phoenix during the summer. The greater the air mass inhaled by the engine, the greater the potential power from the engine.

| Altitude | Horsepower | Horsepower Loss |
|---|---|---|
| 6000 | 400.0000 | 0.0000 |
| 6328 | 396.0000 | 4.0000 |
| 6656 | 392.0400 | 3.9600 |
| 6984 | 388.1196 | 3.9204 |
| 7312 | 384.2384 | 3.8812 |
| 7640 | 380.3960 | 3.8424 |
| 7968 | 376.5921 | 3.8040 |
| 8296 | 372.8261 | 3.7659 |
| 8624 | 369.0979 | 3.7283 |
| 8952 | 365.4069 | 3.6910 |
| 9280 | 361.7528 | 3.6541 |
| 9608 | 358.1353 | 3.6175 |
| 9936 | 354.5539 | 3.5814 |
| 10264 | 351.0084 | 3.5455 |
| 10592 | 347.4983 | 3.5101 |
| 10920 | 344.0233 | 3.4750 |
| 11248 | 340.5831 | 3.4402 |
| 11576 | 337.1773 | 3.4058 |
| 11904 | 333.8055 | 3.3718 |
| 12232 | 330.4674 | 3.3381 |
| 12560 | 327.1628 | 3.3047 |
| 12888 | 323.8911 | 3.2716 |
| 13216 | 320.6522 | 3.2389 |
| 13544 | 317.4457 | 3.2065 |
| 13872 | 314.2713 | 3.1745 |
| 14200 | 311.1285 | 3.1427 |

low from Indianapolis who was convinced that moisture made the air heavier. True, perhaps, but it misses the point. The constituent of the air we are concerned about is oxygen. The *Automotive Handbook* states, "Damp air contains less oxygen than dry air and thus reduces engine power. This power drop is generally negligible. The humidity of the damp, hot air in the tropics can noticeably reduce engine power."

Relative humidity is a familiar term to most people. It is a term you hear every night on the local weather broadcast. Relative humidity describes the amount of water vapor there is in the air. When the temperature of the air increases by 20 degrees F, its ability to hold moisture doubles. This means that when the temperature rises from 60 degrees to 100 degrees F, the amount of moisture the air can hold increases by four times. This is

This is all well and good, but what does it have to do with intake or exhaust systems? To create the maximum amount of power, the engine needs to get the maximum amount of air. The intake manifold restricts and limits the amount of air an engine can get. This problem is amplified when the atmospheric conditions are less than ideal. When the atmospheric conditions are less than ideal the intake manifold and exhaust system must be as close to ideal as possible.

## Humidity

Humidity is the least understood of the atmospheric conditions that affect air, airflow, and power. I once participated in a train-the-trainer where there was a very heated discussion of the effects of humidity on air density. The instructor was a fel-

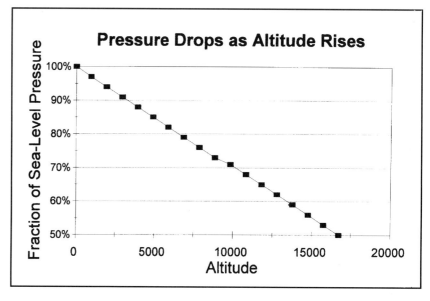

As the altitude increases the air exerts less force on everything it surrounds. Therefore, when the intake valve opens there is less air pressure to force the air into the combustion chamber. With less force, less air enters the combustion chamber and and less power is created by the engine.

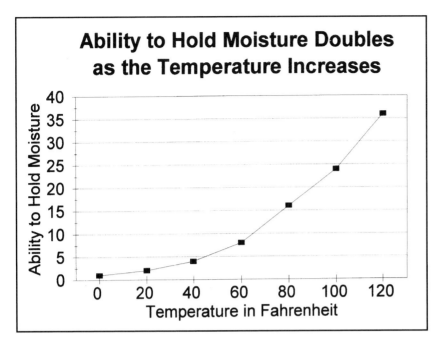

## Ability to Hold Moisture Doubles as the Temperature Increases

*(chart: y-axis "Ability to Hold Moisture" 0–40; x-axis "Temperature in Fahrenheit" 0–120)*

When the temperature of the air increases its ability to hold moisture increases. In fact the ability of the air to hold moisture doubles with every 20 degrees Fahrenheit the temperature increases. Therefore, on a very hot, very humid day, the potential power

from the engine will noticeably decreased. This is why during qualifying at Indy the drivers and crews are all hoping for bright sunshine for their adversaries' qualifying runs and for the sun to pass behind a cloud during their own qualifying run.

der when the intake valve closes is only 50 percent of atmospheric pressure, the volumetric efficiency of the engine is 50 percent. The volumetric efficiency of every engine will vary as the engine speed varies. Intake manifold design, exhaust system design, cylinder head design and cam design are among the factors that will affect the pressure in the cylinder when the intake valve closes. If the engine is running at sea level on the theoretical perfect day the engine will be operating at 100 percent volumetric efficiency when they are filled to 29.92 inches of mercury pressure (a little more than 14.7 pounds per square inch absolute pressure).

why, on an extremely hot, humid day, the moisture in the air can affect the power from the engine.

### Air mass per unit of volume

Air mass per unit of volume is a function of air temperature, air pressure, and humidity. All of these things affect the air mass in each cubic foot of air entering the engine. The ideal situation would be 0 percent relative humidity, -40 degrees F and a drag strip near the Dead Sea. Under these conditions you could get maximum power from your engine. Everything that alters these "ideal" conditions reduces the potential power of the engine.

If the day is hot, the air is less dense, so there will be fewer expandable air molecules in the air mass entering the engine. Power is reduced. In the summer of 1989 it was so hot in Phoenix, Arizona, that jets could not cre-

ate enough thrust to get off the ground. Atmospheric pressure reduces power at the rate of 1 percent every 328 feet. Humidity reduces power. The higher the relative humidity the less power potential there is from the engine. The actual amount of moisture in the air at a given relative humidity doubles for every 20 F the temperature increases. Therefore the effects of humidity are far more noticeable when the humidity is high on a hot day.

The bottom line is: avoid racing on the top of Pikes Peak when the temperature is 90 degrees Fahrenheit and the relative humidity is 99 percent.

### Engine air requirements
### Volumetric efficiency

Volumetric efficiency is the ability of the engine to fill each cylinder with air pressurized to the current atmospheric pressure. If the pressure of the cylin-

### Theoretical airflow

The amount of air drawn in by the engine increases as the size of the engine increases and as the speed of the engine increases. Here is the formula for theoretical airflow:

$$\text{theoretical airflow} = \frac{\text{rpm x displacement}}{3456}$$

Using this formula we find the rat motor I dream about putting into my Volvo 544 would have a theoretical airflow of:

$$\text{theoretical airflow} = \frac{4000 \times 454}{3456}$$

$$\text{theoretical airflow} = \frac{1{,}816{,}000}{3456}$$

$$\text{theoretical airflow} = 525.63 \text{ cfm}$$

This would actually seem disappointing for those who just laid out $500 or more for a Holley 1100 to put on top of their 454.

The job of the intake system is to ensure that the engine can draw in from the atmosphere all the air it could demand under any operating conditions and at any speed. The job of the exhaust system is to ensure that the engine can push out all the waste gases created through the

The conception that a big carburetor, or several big carburetors can increase power is true to an extent. The carburetor is the main point of restriction in the intake system. The bigger the holes in the carburetor, the bigger the throttle bores, the more air can move through the carburetor. Also, the bigger the throttle bores the faster the air flow rate cna change when the throttle position is changed. The reality, however, is that unless the engine is properly prepared to use the extra air flow the $1500+ intake and carburetor system on this engine is a waste.

The Quad 4 engine of General Motors is a 4 valve per cylinder engine. Datasheets showing the results of intake air flow on stock Quad 4 engines indicate that it is capable of 100 percent volumetric efficiency at one point in the RPM throttle position curve.

process of combustion, no matter what the engine operating conditions or engine speed might be.

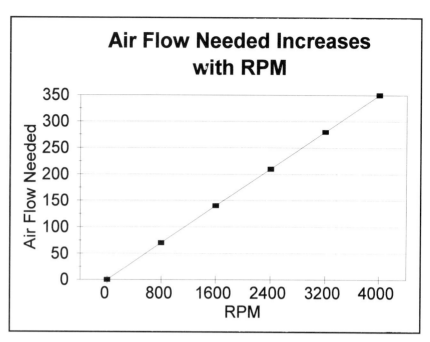

As the engine RPM increases the engine needs to be able to draw in additional air. Although the volume of air gulped by each cylinder on each intake is virtually the same at all engine speeds, the greater the number of intake strokes per minute, the greater the requirement for unrestricted air flow through the intake system.

Theoretical airflow assumes that every engine has a 100 percent volumetric efficiency. Without turbocharging or supercharging any engine will only enjoy 100 percent or more volumetric efficiency within a very narrow range of operation if at all. In the ideal world each cylinder of an internal combustion engine would be like a gentleman's belt. When a man buys a new belt, a belt selected so there will be a couple of unused notches near the end of the belt, one law of physics and the universe always comes into play.

Physical law of the universe #1: The size of a man's waist will always expand so that the last notch of his longest belt will be used. Thus a man's waist with respect to his belts shall always achieve 100 percent volumetric efficiency.

The cylinders of the internal combustion engine are not at all like this. Most engines never achieve 100 percent volumetric efficiency; those that do achieve it do so only in a very narrow rpm band.

## Actual airflow

The actual airflow into an engine and its volumetric efficiency are impossible to determine mathematically; they must be determined through experimentation and measurement. Many modern engines have very good volumetric efficiency. The general Motors Quad 4 engine, for example, makes use of excellent scavenging characteristics of the exhaust system to "supercharge" the intake. As the exhaust gases flow out of the combustion chamber they create a lower pressure there than would be developed by the piston pushing the gases out alone. This helps to draw the intake air charge into the combustion chamber. Additionally the flow of the exhaust gases helps to create an inertial movement of the intake gases which further helps to draw them into the combustion chambers. Because the intake and exhaust systems are so well tuned to one another the engine achieves high volumetric efficiency at several engine speeds.

Generally it is accepted that in practice an engine designed and built for street operation will have a volumetric efficiency of 85 percent. On the other hand, an engine built for racing use, but not equipped with a supercharger, will have a volumetric efficiency of 110 percent.

$$\text{street cfm} = \frac{\text{rpm x displacement}}{3456} \times 0.85$$

$$\text{street cfm} = \frac{4000 \times 454}{3456} \times 0.85$$

$$\text{street cfm} = \frac{1,816,000}{3456} \times 0.85$$

$$\text{street cfm} = 525 \times 0.85$$

$$\text{street cfm} = 446$$

$$\text{racing cfm} = \frac{\text{rpm x displacement}}{3456} \times 1.1$$

$$\text{racing cfm} = \frac{4000 \times 454}{3456} \times 1.1$$

$$\text{racing cfm} = \frac{1,816,000}{3456} \times 1.1$$

$$\text{racing cfm} = 525 \times 1.1$$

$$\text{racing cfm} = 578$$

Air flow is essential to power. As an example of one extreme, I was once working as a technician

A well planned engine, careful attention to detail, an avoidance of using parts just because they looks fast, can yield an engine capable of filling each cylinder to greater than 100 percent volumetric efficiency.

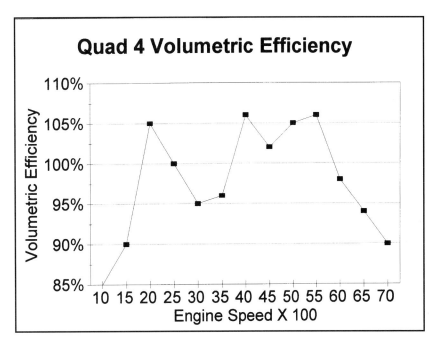

The Quad 4 engine of general motors was introduced in the latter half of the 1980's. One of its more unique characteristics is its rather high level of volumetric efficiency throughout the RPM band. Notice that the volumetric efficiency exceeds 100 percent at several engine speeds.

in an import car repair shop near Seattle, Washington. We had a customer come in with the complaint that his Subaru had a top speed of less than 30 miles per hour (mph). The car had already been into several dealerships and independent shops in the area. An amazing list of what had been done was quoted to me, including rebuilding the carburetor, replacing the spark plugs, replacing the fuel filter, and even servicing the transmission. The problem was Mount St. Helens volcanic ash clogging the air filter. Without the airflow there was no power, without the power the top speed was extremely low. Air flow is power.

## Reducing pressure in the intake system (vacuum)

When a piston is pulled down in a cylinder it creates a low pressure area. During the brief time I worked as an electronics technician many years ago I became familiar with the "solder sucker." This is a solder removal tool that creates a vacuum by using a spring to force a piston through a cylinder. The rapid movement of the piston in the cylinder would create a vacuum that would lift heated, liquid solder off an electrical connection. A piston traveling in a cylinder does not have a spring pushing it but it does have another piston driving it. Let us use the example of a four-cylinder engine. In the typical in-line four-cylinder engine the number one and the number four cylinders travel together. They are called companion cylinders, when one is on the intake stroke the other is on the power stroke. It is, therefore, the piston on the power stroke that replaces the "solder suckers" spring to drive the piston on the intake stroke. When cylinder number one fires the number one piston is driven down by the expanding gases, as it travels down power is transmitted to the crankshaft which in turn pulls the number four piston down its cylinder. As the number four pis-

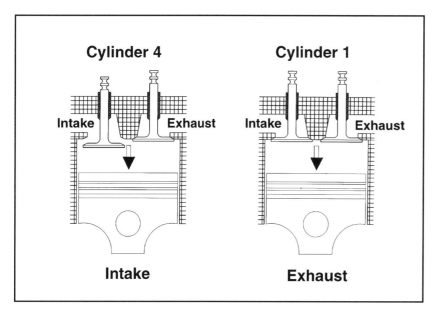

**Cylinder 4**

Intake          Exhaust

**Intake**

**Cylinder 1**

Intake          Exhaust

**Exhaust**

The example above is a typical four cylinder engine. When the piston in cylinder number one is forced down by the rapidly expanding gases that result from combustion, the piston in cylinder number 4 is dragged along with it creating a low pressure area in the cylinder. If the intake valve is open, air from the outside will fill the cylinder. If the volume of air entering the cylinder by the time the piston reaches bottom dead center is equal to cylinder volume then that cylinder is operating with 100 percent volumetric efficiency.

cury). These are pressure readings. The typical motorhead is more familiar with vacuum readings. If the atmospheric pressure is 23in mercury and the pressure in the manifold is 7.7in mercury then:

> vacuum= atmosphere pressure -
> manifold pressure
> vacuum = 23 - 7.7
> vacuum = 15.3

An engine that produces a pressure differential of 20in mercury at sea level will only produce a pressure differential of 15.3in mercury at Donner Summit. The result of this loss of pressure differential is a loss of force to push the air into the cylinder as the piston retreats. With less force, less air enters the cylinder and there is a lower potential for power.

On a more motorhead friendly planet, such as Venus with a 21 percent oxygen atmosphere, the atmospheric pressure would be higher. On Venus the atmospheric pressure is 1,352psi, 90 times that of planet Earth. That means that the estimated pressure differential would be 892 psi. Wow, that would be like running 877 pounds (lb) of boost on your turbocharger. Can you imagine a 40 horse Volkswagen that could turn low 5's in the quarter-mile! Of course there is the question of aerodynamics in that thick atmosphere, but that is a topic for another book.

ton travels down its cylinder the volume of the cylinder that can be filled by air is increased, if the intake valve remains closed (which it should not) the pressure in that cylinder would drop quite low. If the intake valve opens (which it should) the low pressure area created by the number four piston will be filled with air.

To ensure that the drop in pressure caused by the retreating piston occurs, it is necessary that there be good cylinder integrity. A leaking head gasket, worn rings or poorly sealing valves can interfere with the low pressure created by the piston, or pull other substances into the cylinder. It is necessary to ensure proper air/fuel ratio that all of the air entering the engine be measured air, air that has been detected by whatever type of air measuring device the engine employs. Because of this it is essential that all of the air destined for the cylinder be air that

passes through the common area of the intake manifold.

It is really too bad that Venus does not have a 21 percent oxygen atmosphere like planet Earth. In a typical internal combustion engine we are lucky to reduce the pressure in the intake system to 1/3 that of atmospheric. The action of the pistons in the cylinder, therefore, only creates a pressure differential ("vacuum") of 10 psi (20in mercury) at sea level when the engine is idling. As the altitude increases and atmospheric pressure drops, the difference between atmospheric pressure and intake manifold pressure at an idle remains at a relatively constant 3:1 ratio. When you cross over Donner Pass in California (altitude 7200 feet), the atmospheric pressure is about 11 1/2psi (about 23in mercury). The pressure in the intake manifold is about 3 3/4psi (about 7.7in mer-

### Valve action

The four stroke engine common to the automobile today was the brainchild of the 19th century engineer N.A. Otto or 19th century French engineer De Rochas (depending on which side you take in the lawsuit between these two gentlemen that took place in 1876). The four strokes used in this type of engine are intake, compression, ignition and exhaust. I like to think of them as suck, squeeze, boom, belch. The

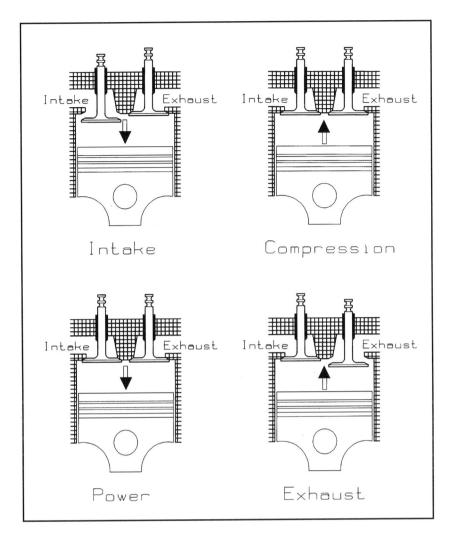

Intake

Compression

Power

Exhaust

On the intake stroke the piston moves down the cylinder creating a low pressure area in the cylinder. At the same time the intake valve is opened by the camshaft. Air rushes in to fill the low pressure area. When the piston reaches the bottom of the intake stroke, the intake valve closes and the piston begins its journey up the cylinder. As the piston travels up the cylinder it compresses the air in the cylinder, this creates heat to help with combustion and to improve the exiting of the air molecules when

opening and closing of the valves is controlled by the camshaft and must be precisely synchronized with the rotation of the crankshaft. On the intake stroke the intake valve must be open and be the sole path for air to enter the cylinder. On the compression

combustion does occur. After ignition of the air/fuel charge the piston is driven down by the exploding force. This is called the power stroke. As the piston approaches bottom dead center the exhaust valve is opened by the camshaft. Soon the piston will begin its upward journey on the exhaust stroke. The piston will sweep the cylinder clean of the combustion gas residue. The cylinder is now ready to receive fresh air on the next intake stroke.

stroke the valves must seal the air/fuel charge in. This is important for the exhaust valve but it is even more important for the intake valve. Potential power will be lost as the piston rises on the compression stroke. Some of the pressurizing gas in the combus-

tion chamber will escape into the intake manifold. This will pressurize the intake manifold and reduce the pressure differential between the intake and the atmosphere. This will impede air flow. During the power stroke this same leaking valve will pass the expanding gases of combustion into the manifold. Since these gases are much greater in volume their potential effect will be even more devastating the those forced into the manifold during the compression stroke.

## Scavenging

The dictionary defines "scavenge" as: 1. To remove filth, rubbish and refuse from... 2. To remove exhaust gases from... Both of these definitions are appropriate. This topic has to do with the efficiency with which the exhaust system cleans the cylinder before the intake system begins to refill it.

The exhaust valve opens just prior to the piston reaching bottom dead center (BDC). At this point the gases in the combustion chamber are still at an extremely high pressure. Between the moment of exhaust valve opening and BDC almost 50 percent of the combusted gases leave the combustion chamber, forced out by their own pressure. As the piston travels up during the exhaust stroke it pushes most of the remaining gases out of the cylinder. When the piston approaches top dead center (TDC) the intake valve opens. By this time the exhaust gases have considerable momentum. At this point both the intake and the exhaust valves are open. This is called valve overlap or gas exchange TDC. The inertia of the exiting exhaust gases helps to draw in the intake air charge.

## Pressurizing the intake system
### Dynamic supercharging

When the average person talks about supercharging they imagine a big blower sitting on

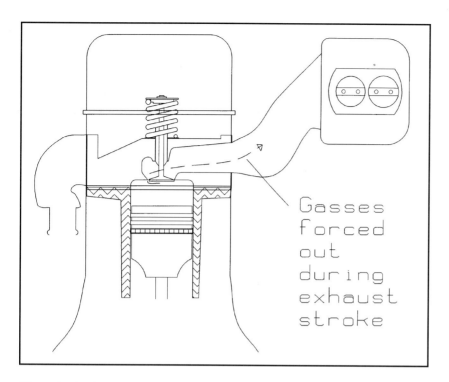

Gasses forced out during exhaust stroke

top of the engine. They imagine Don Garlits (is my age showing?) sitting behind a monster "gimmy" blower with flames shooting out of the exhaust (yes my age is definitely reflected in this). In reality dynamic supercharging involves a much more subtle approach. Dynamic supercharging maximizes the use of the 100mi column of air to force the air into the cylinders. There are two types of dynamic supercharging: ram pipe supercharging and tuned-intake tube charging.

### Ram pipe supercharging

In this technology each cylinder has its own intake manifold

When the intake valve leaks exhaust gases into the intake manifold the pressure in the intake manifold rises. A higher pressure in the intake manifold results in less pressure differential between the intake system and the atmosphere. The result is less power from the engine.

Below:Rampipe supercharging technology gives each cylinder its own intake manifold usually connected to a common receiver. This design uses the kinetic energy of the gas moving into the cylinder to press the air into the cylinder.

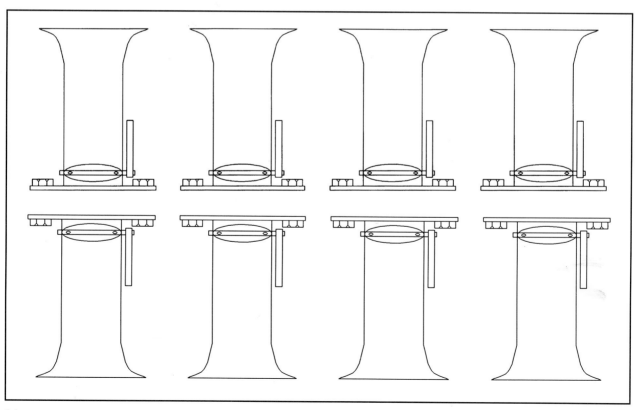

usually connected to a common receiver. This design uses the kinetic energy of the gas moving into the cylinder to press the air into the cylinder. In a sense it uses the air as a "mallet" to pound the air into the cylinder.

## Tuned intake tube charging

This intake system is just like the ram pipe system except the intake runners are grouped together by ignition interval.

## Turbocharging

Turbocharging is a fascinating technology and will be covered thoroughly later in the book. Essentially a turbocharger takes energy that would have gone out the tailpipe as heat and converts it into energy. The energy then drives a turbine that spins a compressor. The compressor increases the pressure in the intake manifold. The air molecules become squashed together cramming more oxygen molecules into the cylinders. Since more air in the cylinders translates directly as more power from the engine this is a very efficient way to increase the power output of an engine. Some turbocharged engines run over 100 psi of boosts. This means that the mass of air in the cylinders can be over six times greater than without a turbocharger. This means that the power potential of the engine is many times greater than without the turbocharger. Of course all good things do have a downside. When the boost pressures are this high the engines have a very short life expectancy, perhaps seconds.

## Supercharging

A supercharger is an engine-driven pump used to force air into the cylinders. This is a topic that will be covered later in this book as well. Engine- driven superchargers are what people typically think of when the subject of superchargers comes up.

Supercharging will be discussed more thoroughly later in this book.

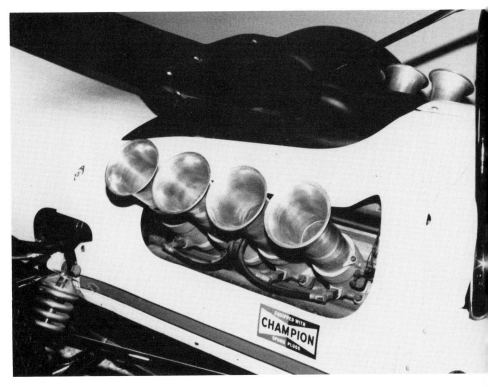

The rampipe intake supercharging technique was very popular in the 1960s. This old formula car is typical of those admired by those of us who grew up thinking that James Garner gave up gambling in the old west for driving Formula I in Europe.

## Air fuel ratio
## Theoretically correct air fuel ratio (stoichiometry)

Gasoline is a complex mixture of hydrocarbons containing approximately 86 percent carbon and 14 percent hydrogen by weight. There are also trace impurities which contribute to the noxious soup from the tailpipe. Sulfur can combine with oxygen during the combustion process producing sulfuric acid and sulfur dioxide. There is also a wide range of additives that are used.

Until recently tetraethyl lead or tetramethyl lead were used as knock inhibitors. When these oxidized in the combustion chamber they not only produced an acid but also contributed to the lead contamination of the environment.

As odd as it may sound, the air itself is one of its own prime defilers. About 78 percent of the air we breath is nitrogen. When this nitrogen is combined with oxygen during the combustion process it can produce both nitrogen monoxide and nitrogen dioxide.

Air is made up of 78 percent nitrogen and 21 percent oxygen. The remaining 1 percent consists of various trace gases such as xenon, neon and argon.

The perfect mix of fuel and air is 14.7 parts of air by weight to one part of fuel, by weight. When mixed in these proportions there will be theoretically no air and no fuel left at the end of combustion. In fact in theory there will only be carbon dioxide ($CO_2$), nitrogen and water. We will see later that this is not the reality.

## Keeping the charge in suspension

When it comes to mixing fuel and air there are two basic types of intake manifolds—wet mani-

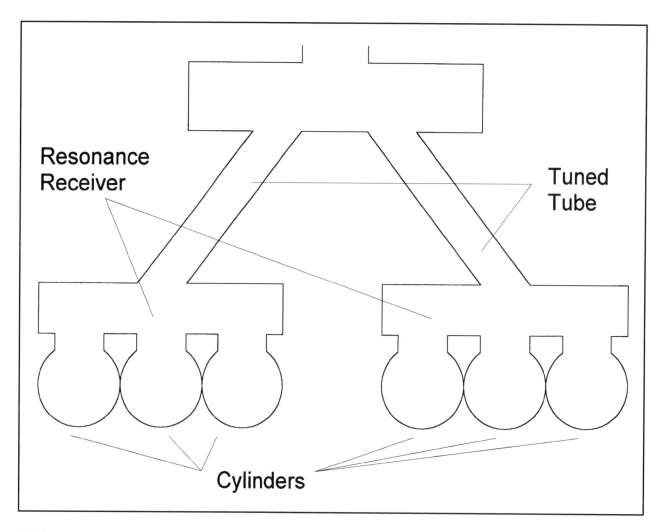

Resonance Receiver

Tuned Tube

Cylinders

This intake system is just like the ram pipe system except the intake runners are grouped together by ignition interval.

folds and dry manifolds. Actually, for a gasoline spark ignition engine the concept of a "dry manifold" is not strictly correct. Even in these manifolds the air and fuel are mixed just above the intake valve. Only direct injected engines, engines where the fuel is injected directly into the combustion chamber, are true dry manifold engines.

This may be where the real trick lies. Wet manifold engines use carburetor(s) or throttle body injection to mix the fuel with the air destined for the combustion chambers. As the air/fuel charge moves through the intake runners there is a tendency for some of the fuel to drop out of suspension. Imagine a mountain stream for a moment. As the rushing waters come to level ground they slow, and as they slow rocks begin to drop from the moving water. The slower the waters move, the smaller the rocks that will drop out of suspension. The same thing happens in an intake manifold. Fuel particles will drop out of suspension as the airflow through the intake slows. This drop out is held to a minimum on multipoint injected engines. These "dry manifold" engines mix the fuel with the flowing air only just above the intake valve. As a result the fuel is more evenly and accurately carried to the cylinder.

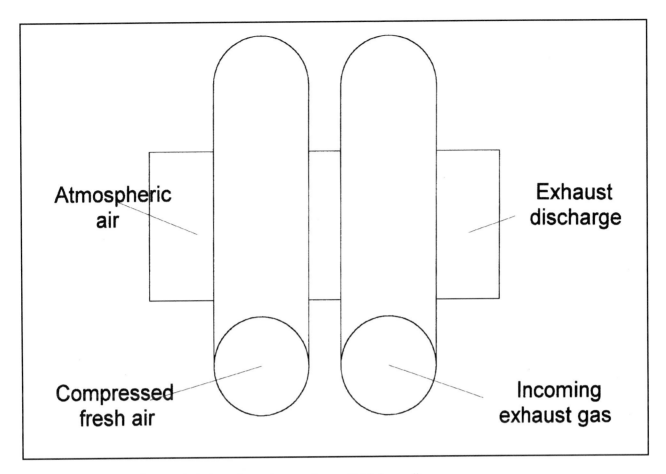

Atmospheric air

Exhaust discharge

Compressed fresh air

Incoming exhaust gas

Turbochargers have a long and glorious record for making cars go fast. Although this record dates back to the 1920's, they did not become extremely popular until high quality, high speed, inexpensive bearings became available in the 1950's.

# Gasses in the Atmosphere

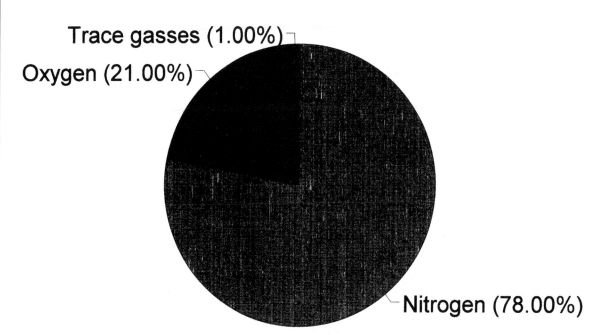

Trace gasses (1.00%)

Oxygen (21.00%)

Nitrogen (78.00%)

The atmosphere is made up of gases that provide almost the perfect performance blend. Twenty-one percent of the air is oxygen, a suitable amount for oxidizing the fuel. Seventy-eight percent of the air is nitrogen, this provides a largely inert gas to be expanded when combustion occurs.

Next page: Superchargers were popular on both racecars and street cars during the 1920's and 1930's. However, with the advent of the "big iron" V-8's of the 1950's they became relagated to running a quarter mile at a time.

A wet intake manifold carries the fuel and air from the mixer, carburetor or throttle body injection system, to the intake valve as a mixture. Any place where the velocity of the air slows there is a risk of the fuel falling out of suspension. If this occurs, the cylinder will fire lean.

Although the term "dry manifold" is somewhat inaccurate, it means that the fuel and air are mixed at the last moment before entering the cylinder, just above the intake valve.

# Chapter 2

# Air Intake System Components

## The Intake Ducting

In many climates, good maintenance of the intake air ducting may be the cheapest and easiest thing you can do to ensure peak power and performance. Back in the days when "Saturday Night Live" was entertaining, Chrysler introduced the Lean Burn system. This system featured a computer that hung on the side of the air cleaner. Inside the computer was a very large, heat producing transistor that controlled the operation of the ignition coil. In order to keep the computer cool, cold air was routed by a tube from the radiator bulkhead to the air cleaner. When this tube was removed the computer had a tendency to overheat.

## When it is important

I know that my average reader is too intelligent to own a Lean Burn car. However, if the air coming through this fresh air tube from the radiator bulkhead can be used to cool a computer, is it not logical that this air must be significantly cooler than the air under the hood? And if cooler air is denser air, and if denser air means improved performance, then it must be worth the few dollars it takes to maintain or replace this hose.

## When it is not important

About the only time it could be said that the fresh air tube is not important is when the only consideration is performance and the tube forms a restriction. If the restriction of the tube is greater than the benefit gained by the cooler air then the tube should be eliminated. However, keep in mind that often a tube that appears to be restrictive ac-

As unimportant as it may appear, the fresh air tube has many important functions. It serves to insure that the engine receives cool air instead of warm under-hood air. It may also form a resonance chamber that will improve air flow into the engine. In this picture the "insignificant" fresh air tube runs between the alternator and the windshield washer bottle.

tually acts as a resonance chamber. This resonance chamber improves airflow into the intake system. Removing the tube might reduce performance instead of improve it. Additionally, in many jurisdictions removing the fresh air tube may be illegal.

## Air cleaner/filter

The air cleaner shares the dubious honor of being the engine's primary line of defense against airborne contaminants and being the first point of serious air restriction in the intake system. Although we seldom really think about it, airborne grit, sand and other abrasives can destroy an engine very quickly.

There is a story that I heard from some civilian Marine Corps mechanics. I do not know if it is true, but it does paint an excellent picture of the importance of the air filtration system. It seems that there was a training session on the maintenance of diesel engines. The preventative maintenance was done, then, as a treat, the trainees were allowed to drive the vehicles through the desert areas of Twenty-Nine Palms Marine Base. Unfortunately the trainer failed to emphasize that the air filters needed to be reinstalled before the joy ride. Several engines were destroyed by the sand.

Now I love oxymorons. You know, phrases like "military intelligence," "jumbo shrimp" and the like. One of the best oxymorons in the automotive indus-

The odd thing about air filters is that, in general, the better they work, the worse they work. Filtering contaminants from the air is done by forcing the air through a fine screen of paper, foam or gauze. The finer the filter, the better it works, but the finer the filter the more the filter inhibits air flow. On the other hand, the more open the filter pores are the freer the air flows, but the more contaminants get through.

try is the term "free-flow air filter." Of course this may be a matter of interpretation. All air filters should be free-flowing, free-flowing to the maximum requirements of the engine. Those of you who grew up, as I did, in the world when teenagers' popular entertainment was limited to drag racing and beach parties, are very familiar with the idea of monster carburetors. I can actually remember having a serious conversation about whether or not to "put a Holley 1150cfm" on a 289ci engine. The amount of air actually inhaled by an engine is usually much less than what pride or desire would like. In general the airflow rate through the air filtration element should be 15-20 times the displacement of one cylinder. It may seem that the number of cylinders should be taken into account for the 15-20 times rule. Keep in mind however that only one cylinder has an open intake valve and is drawing air at any time. The air filter need only flow sufficiently for one cylinder.

## Construction of the typical factory air cleaner

The typical factory air cleaner has provision for performing three jobs—it filters the air, mixes warm air and cold, and dampens noise. Air filtration will be discussed later, let us look at warm air mixing and noise.

## Warm air mixing

Okay, people in Minnesota listen up, people in Guam take a snooze. It is no secret that warm air will hold fuel in suspension better than cold air. There is no doubt that pre-warmed air will also be easier to "burn" once inside the combustion chamber. Anyone that has ever tried to start a car in Minneapolis in December and then tried in Guam a few days later can confirm this. There is more to this than just the inconvenience of poor driveability when the engine is cold. Any cylinders in which the air is not warm enough to support proper combustion will not fire properly; any cylinder that is not firing properly will be a heavy polluter.

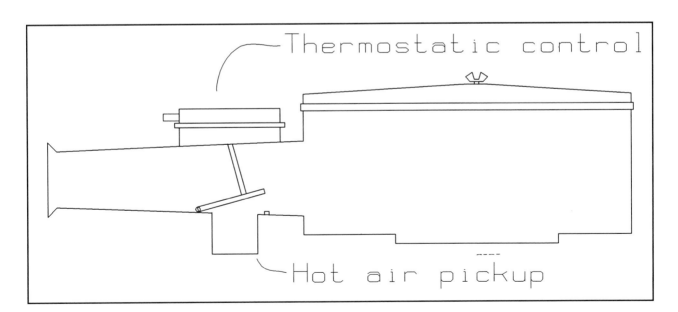

Thermostatic control

Hot air pickup

Most factory air cleaners are equipped with a "heated air door." When the underhood temperature is low, the air being pulled in through the intake system has a poor ability

to hold gasoline in suspension. The cool air also has poor combustion characteristics. The thermostatic air cleaner pulls air from the exhaust manifold and mixes it with the cold air

under the hood. Removing or disabling the this function can severely affect driveability and emissions.

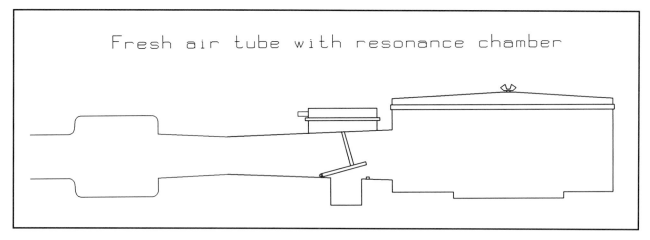

Fresh air tube with resonance chamber

Reduction of intake noise is a concern of the designers of factory air cleaners. Keeping the noise to a minimum is no accident. It is engineered.

Once the engine is started, the exhaust manifold will warm up very quickly. Many factory air cleaners take advantage of this heat. The heat is captured through a heat resistant metal or metalized paper tube. The warmer air coming through this tube is then mixed with air coming through the main air inlet of the air cleaner. At the point where the air from this tube joins the main body of air entering the engine there is a control door. This door is intended to cut off the warm air when the ambient temperature or coolant temperature is above a predetermined point. If the air entering the intake system is warmer than it needs to be there can be a loss of power. Warm air is air that has been expanded. Therefore, if the temperature of the air is higher than it really needs to be to meet the goal of low emissions and good warm driveability, there will be a proportional power loss.

## Noise

In the early eighties I began teaching electronic engine controls to automotive fleet maintenance personnel. One of the things I observed early on was that most of the police cars that came in for service had the top of the air cleaner inverted. I thought it odd that intelligent police officers could believe inverting the top of the air cleaner could improve power. For years I sought a more believable answer to this mystery. After years of questioning technicians and police officers I finally obtained a satisfactory answer. Imagine that you are cruising a dangerous neighborhood. You turn down a dark alley in pursuit of a perpetrator. With the air cleaner lid turned upside down, the air flowing through the carburetor will yield a deep, throaty roar. The hope is that this roar will intimidate the perpetrator.

This story emphasizes the second important job that the air cleaner must do... silence the sound created by several hundred cubic feet of air per minute entering the engine. Although the typical performance-minded individual usually cares little about intake noise, it should be pointed out that the typical manufacturer also does not care much about this noise.

The sound of 300-400 cubic feet of air per minute being pulled through a couple of holes only slightly bigger than a half dollar can be very annoying to the average car owner. Remember the eighties? Remember yup-pies? Can you imagine courting a potential junk-bond client in a car that goes "wonnnnn" every time you step on the accelerator? It would be enough to fry the client's sushi.

The manufacturers expend a great deal of effort trying to reduce the noise created by the induction of air. While this is done in large part for the comfort and convenience of the driver and passengers there are state, local and federal regulations governing noise pollution. In fact, for big rigs—over the road trucks and the like—there are very strict Environmental Protection Agency rules concerning intake noise.

The bottom line concerning sound is that if you decide to replace the air cleaner assembly, expect the noise to increase. When the engineer designed the original air cleaner for this application, he did not just reach up on the shelf and pull one off. He got out his slide rule and began by estimating the speed of sound in the air where the vehicle is going to be operated. He measured the length of the intake runners, the mean diameter of the intake manifold, and the air filter volume. Then he was ready to calculate the resonant frequency of the intake system.

$$\text{frequency} = \frac{\frac{\text{speed of sound}}{2\pi}}{\sqrt{\frac{\text{intake mean cross section}}{\text{length of intake* filter volume}}}} *$$

## Emission laws and the air cleaner

Since the seventies the air cleaner assembly has been an integral part of the emission control system. In many jurisdictions across the country replacing the air cleaner with some aftermarket air cleaners may be blatantly illegal. The toughest jurisdiction in the United States is California. There are only a very few street-legal changes allowed for in the State of California Air Resources Board document Reference Number A-92-443, "Modifications to Motor Vehicle Engine and Emission Control Systems Exempted Under Vehicle Code Section 27156." If the vehicle you are modifying is destined for the street, be sure to confirm that the new air cleaner you are purchasing has been approved by your state.

Although you may feel, and may even be able to prove, that the new air cleaner does not affect emissions in the least, you will still have to convince the emissions inspector or referee. There will be more about aftermarket air cleaners a little later in this chapter.

## Filter elements

An area where a great deal of improvement can be made without severe legal restrictions is the air filter element. The paper filter used by the manufacturer when the car or truck is assembled usually supplies adequate filtration....just adequate. You may find this hard to believe, but one of the primary considerations of the manufacturers when they select or design an air filtration element is cost. For some reason they consider it important to save a few dollars per car and therefore save a few million dollars per year in manufacturing costs. I think that is called capitalism or something. In many cases a replacement air filter is of lower quality than the original.

To a certain extent air filtration is a "Catch 22" situation. To provide good filtration the filter element must filter out all particles capable of damaging the engine. In general, the tinier the particle a given element can filter, the more that filter restricts airflow.

The first car I owned was a Volkswagen with a 1200cc engine. This car had an oil bath air filter. Very popular during the first half of the century, the oil bath filter trapped particles in a tub of oil. These are expensive to manufacture and expensive to install on the assembly line.

The most common air filter element in the automotive industry today is the paper air filter. This is one of those areas where it can be said that every filter manufacturer makes the best air filter. It is difficult for me to recommend a particular manufacturer. Ask your local mechanic or auto parts man which brand he would recommend.

There are a wide range of performance air filters available. These range from paper, to foam, to oil-impregnated foam, to gauze, to combinations of these.

My first experience with performance air filters was during the seventies when the shop I worked in made a specialty of installing Weber carburetors. The air filter we used was a relatively coarse foam with an oil spray coating. There are several of these on the market currently as replacement cartridges.

This may look like a hot set up, and it may be, however there are two things the builder should have kept in mind. First this air filtration system has no way of reducing intake air noise. This is probably of little importance to the owner. More important than the noise is the fact that the scoop is drawing air directly from the radiator air flow path. This air will be heated, expanded and inherently contain less potential power than it would if the scoop were higher and protruded through the hood of the car.

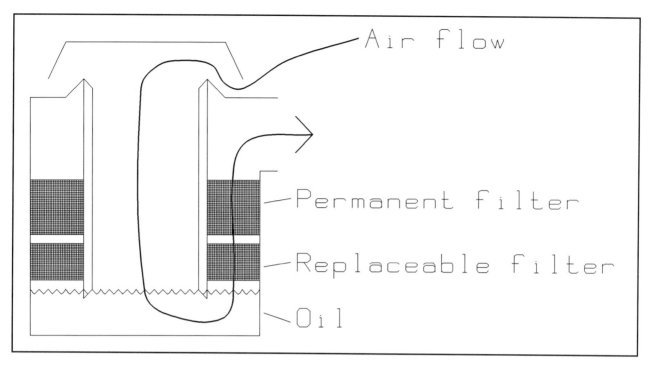

Air flow

Permanent filter

Replaceable filter

Oil

The oil bath air filter was very popular during the early part of the century in automotive applications. Offering very good filtration ability, the oil bath filter remains popular in the trucking industry.

Paper, foam, and gauze filters all begin life with good airflow and filtration characteristics. The paper filter, however, suffers a rapid decline in airflow capability as it filters the air. The dust and contamination particles build up rapidly on its surface. The paper filter is a single plane filter. The airflow through the filter decreases at the same rate as the trapping of contaminants.

The foam filter features multiple levels of filtration. There are many paths for the air to take through the filter. When a path becomes restricted there are many other paths for the air to take. These filters are generally "lifetime" filters. They can be cleaned and re-oiled many times.

Like the foam air filter, the gauze air filter features multiple paths for airflow. Generally marketed as "lifetime" filters, gauze filters are much like the foam filters in that they can be cleaned and reused many times.

The oil bath air filter was once the standard of the industry.

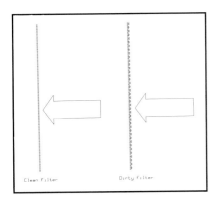

The air flow through a paper filter element decreases rapidly as it does its job. Most any filter starts off new with a good air flow ability, the important issue is how long will it continue to flow well once it begins to collect dirt.

## Aftermarket air cleaners
### Street legal

As was mentioned earlier, the choice of street legal aftermarket air cleaners may be extremely limited. The worse case is California. What follows is a complete list of permitted replacement air cleaners in California as per State of California Air Resources Board document Reference Number A-92-443, "Modifications to Motor Vehicle Engine and Emission Control Systems Exempted Under Vehicle Code Section 27156."

As you can see from the accompanyng table, there are very few applications where replacement air cleaners have been authorized by the state of California. Those of you who are blessed and do not live in California may have a few more options available to you.

### Track only

On the track, except for class restrictions, anything goes. Many weekend and professional racers will opt not to have an air cleaner or filtration system at all. It is hard to sit here at this computer keyboard and criticize someone who is blowing away the competition every Friday and Saturday night. Nevertheless, in most environments there is enough hard particle contamination in the air to do very serious damage to the engine in a very short time. Custom air cleaners are available for virtually any carbureted or throttle body injected engine. Only a few multipoint injected engines have aftermarket air cleaner assemblies available.

### Modifying the factory air cleaner

Most factory air cleaners consist of a shallow tube or pan with a small air inlet cut in the side. A snorkel is usually attached to the air inlet to assist in directing airflow into the air cleaner. Most aftermarket "performance" air cleaners have the walls of the air cleaner tube removed. This allows air to flow from 360 degrees around the throttle assembly. The walls of the air cleaner then become the air filter itself. The air cleaner on most cars is capable of flowing more than the actual airflow of the engine on which it is installed during normal operation. If the car is to be used under circumstances where maximum performance is required, such as racing or trailer towing, then the air cleaner assembly can become a restriction to airflow and therefore performance.

In the old days guys would flip the air cleaner lid upside down. While the effects of doing this were largely psychological it did allow the air to bypass the restriction of the air cleaner inlet snorkel and allow the air to approach the filter equally from all sides. This greatly increased the potential air flow, the question is, did it increase the actual air flow? Probably it did not. The design of fuel injection air cleaners does not make inverting the lid practical or desirable.

The foam air filter works like a multiple layer filtration system. There are many paths for the air to take through the filter. When one path becomes restricted there are other paths still open for the air to take.

| E.O. or Res. Number (Date) | Manufacturer "Product" (Model/Kit No.) | Vehicle Applications |
|---|---|---|
| D-13 (6/15/83) | Adroit Products, Inc. "Power Air Booster" | 66-72 AMC with non-heated inlet air |
| D-13 (6/15/83) | Adroit Products, Inc. "Power Air Booster" | 66-72 Chrysler with non-heated inlet air |
| D-13 (6/15/83) | Adroit Products, Inc. "Power Air Booster" | 66-72 Ford with non-heated inlet air |
| D-13 (6/15/83) | Adroit Products, Inc. "Power Air Booster" | 66-72 GM (except Vega) with non-heated inlet air |
| D-186-4 (4/21/92) | HKS USA, Inc. "Power Flow Air Filter System" Model No. 3333EC | 76864K 86-89 1.6L Acura Integra |
| D-186-4 (4/21/92) | HKS USA, Inc. "Power Flow Air Filter System" Model No. 3333EC | 76965N 90-92 1.8L Acura Integra |
| D-186-4 (4/21/92) | HKS USA, Inc. "Power Flow Air Filter System" Model No. 3333EC | 47373N 90-92 2.0L Eagle Talon/Plymouth Laser/Mitsubishi Eclipse |
| D-186-4 (4/21/92) | HKS USA, Inc. "Power Flow Air Filter System" Model No. 3333EC | 36564M 88-92 1.6L Honda CRX/Civic |
| D-186-4 (4/21/92) | HKS USA, Inc. "Power Flow Air Filter System" Model No. 3333EC | 58182K 86-88 1.3L Mazda RX-7 |
| D-186-4 (4/21/92) | HKS USA, Inc. "Power Flow Air Filter System" Model No. 3333EC | 58182N 88-91 1.3L Mazda RX-7 |
| D-186-4 (4/21/92) | HKS USA, Inc. "Power Flow Air Filter System" Model No. 3333EC | 58686M 88-89 1.6L Mazda 323 GT & GTX |
| D-186-4 (4/21/92) | HKS USA, Inc. "Power Flow Air Filter System" Model No. 3333EC | 59087P 90-92 1.6L Mazda MX-5 Miata |
| D-186-4 (4/21/92) | HKS USA, Inc. "Power Flow Air Filter System" Model No. 3333EC | 58188Q 91-92 1.8L Mazda MX-3 |
| D-186-4 (4/21/92) | HKS USA, Inc. "Power Flow Air Filter System" Model No. 3333EC | 58886P 91-92 1.6L Mercury Capri |
| D-186-4 (4/21/92) | HKS USA, Inc. "Power Flow Air Filter System" Model No. 3333EC | 47573P 91-92 2.0L Mitsubishi Galant |

| E.O. or Res. Number | Manufacturer "Product" (Model/Kit No.) | Vehicle Applications |
|---|---|---|
| D-186-4 (4/21/92) | HKS USA, Inc. "Power Flow Air Filter System" Model No. 3333EC | 24751P 90-92 3.0L Nissan 300ZX |
| D-186-4 (4/21/92) | HKS USA, Inc. "Power Flow Air Filter System" Model No. 3333EC | 24552N 89-90 2.4L Nissan 240ZX |
| D-186-4 (4/21/92) | HKS USA, Inc. "Power Flow Air Filter System" Model No. 3333EC | 11025L 86-92 3.0L Toyota Supra |
| D-186-4 (4/21/92) | HKS USA, Inc. "Power Flow Air Filter System" Model No. 3333EC | 11024L 82-86 2.8L Toyota Supra |
| D-186-4 (4/21/92) | HKS USA, Inc. "Power Flow Air Filter System" Model No. 3333EC | 11026L 87-92 3.0L Toyota Supra Turbo |
| D-186-4 (4/21/92) | HKS USA, Inc. "Power Flow Air Filter System" Model No. 3333EC | 11327P 91-92 2.2L Toyota MR-2 |
| D-186-4 (4/21/92) | HKS USA, Inc. "Power Flow Air Filter System" Model No. 3333EC | 11328P 91-92 2.0L Toyota MR-2 Turbo |
| D-186-4 (4/21/92) | HKS USA, Inc. "Power Flow Air Filter System" Model No. 3333EC | 11333M 88-89 1.6L Toyota MR-2 |

Tuned Port Injection Specialists located in Chaska, Minnesota, has done a lot of experiments with air flow modification on the General Motors Tuned Port Injection system used in the Corvettes, Camaros and Firebirds. One of their publications, *TPS Insider Hints,* documents airflow studies conducted on the air cleaner assembly of the GM 5.7 liter Tuned Port engine. The stock air cleaner with a stock lid and a stock filter was able to flow 648 cfm.

This seems to be a comfortable amount above the 426 estimated cfm for the 350 Tuned Port engine and indeed modification on a stock engine would not be necessary. In fact there is enough airflow capability in the stock air cleaner to handle 6400rpm at 100 percent volumetric efficiency. What this means to the average motorist is that the air cleaner will only become a factor when there is a desire to suddenly change the pressure in the intake manifold.

When the throttle plates are opened there is a sudden increase in the velocity of the air mass entering the intake manifold. Cruising at 2000rpm our sample 350 is only swallowing about 141cfm. When the throttle is matted the demand suddenly jumps to a potential of 434cfm and as the rpm climbs so will the demand. The more open and free-flowing the intake system is both upstream and downstream of the throttle plates the faster an air mass will build, and therefore, the faster torque will build.

TPIS and others make air cleaner housings for the 5.7 and 5.0 Tuned Port applications which boast increased cfm capability and therefore an increased ability to make a sudden change in mass airflow rate. A crude but effective method of accomplishing the same thing is to trim the air filter lid so that all of the air filter is exposed and the airflow through the filter is totally unrestricted by the cover itself.

**Where the fuel is introduced**

As implied earlier, there are two places that the fuel may be introduced into the air stream. Carburetors by their very nature introduce the fuel into the air stream prior to the intake manifold. Many manufacturers, and even aftermarket manufacturers like Holley, are marketing centralized fuel injection systems. More commonly known as "throttle body injection," these injection systems mix the fuel and air prior to the intake manifold, like

29

Many perfromance air filters are permanant filters. Although they need not be replaced on a regular basis, they do need regular maintenance. Some of the filters require special cleaners and oiling.

a carburetor. They have the advantage of being relatively cheap, relatively easy to install, and reasonably precise in their ability to meter fuel.

Many late model applications use multipoint fuel injection. In these systems the fuel is introduced into the airflow stream just above the intake valve. Since all that is traveling through the majority of the intake manifold is air, the design of the manifold is not dictated by the need to keep the air/fuel charge mixed uniformly in the intake.

## Carburetors

The Merriam-Webster Dictionary defines the carburetor as a device used to supply an internal combustion engine with an explosive mixture of fuel and air. The carburetor is seen by most mechanics as representing a day when the technology of the automobile was simpler—a day when the pace of life was a function of how many ice cubes were needed to make your mint-julep drinkable. In reality the carburetor is a frighteningly temperamental piece of equipment. Its proper operation depends on subtle pressure differentials between the fuel bowl and the venturi. I must confess that after twenty years working primarily with fuel injected vehicles, I look at carburetors as something that Columbus would have refused to use on his second voyage to the Americas

The gauze air filter element, like the foam filter, restricts very slowly. There are multiple air flow paths so air flow is maintained at a high level well beyond the time that a paper filter would have impeded performance.

Remove the metal walls around the air filter. Expose as much of the 100 mile tall column of air directly to the filter as possible.

because they were out of date. Of course, this personal prejudice ignores the sophistication of modern carburetors.

The main problems with the carburetor as an air/fuel mixing device are the extreme limitations it places on intake manifold design.

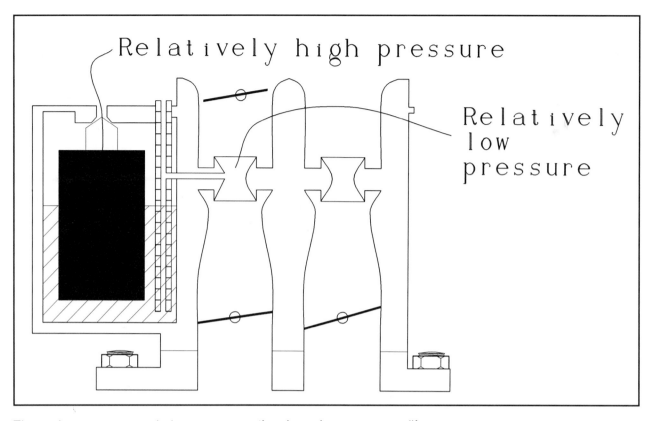

The carburetor may remind most technicians of "the good ol' days," but the reality is a complicated device. Its operation depends on pressure differentials and air flow.

Power carburetors have come a long way in recent decades. For raw power these carburetors still have one advantage over fuel injection. Fuel injection systems respond with a slight delay. This is because most in-jection systems must measure air flow at a point either upstream or downstream of the throttle body. In a carburetor the air measurement is in the throttle body.

# Chapter 3
## ——————Theories of Manifold Design——————

### The Intake Manifold

The intake manifold is the final conduit for getting the air, and sometimes the fuel, to the intake valve. The design of the intake manifold has a great deal to do with the creation and control of horsepower and torque.

### "No-manifold induction systems"

Back in the days when the name Andretti was brand new at Indianapolis, most race cars, except those descended from moonshine runners, had one little stack for each cylinder. To me anything else was just not a race car. In these intake systems each of the cylinders has its own access to the 100mi tall column of air above the engine. The only twists and turns the air has to take on its way to the combustion chamber are the twists and turns in the cylinder head. So far this seems like the ideal intake manifold. However, as with other ideal things there is a problem.

I am reminded of the scene from *Winning* where late at night the ace mechanic is tuning the engine on an Indy car. He fumbles with his hearing aid, revs the engine and says to the driver, "I think number 3 is a bit weak," or something like that. In order to extract peak and equal power out of each of the cylinder, it is necessary that each of the throttle plates open at the same rate to the same position. Unequal movement of the throttle plates will result in unequal power from the various cylinders of the engine. On a race car destined strictly for track use and owned or maintained by someone who finds the thrill of agony and the victory of defeat in the constant tweaking of complex

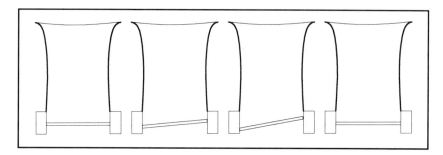

While having a separate air induction tube may seem like a perfect way to get air into the combustion system there is a problem that makes it less than ideal. When the throttle is moved by the driver each of the throttle plates must move at the same rate to the same positions. If the movement of the throttle plates is not synchronized the power output of the cylinders will be uneven.

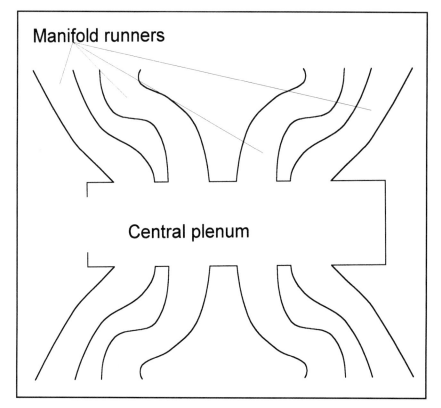

A "manifold" is used to route air from the atmosphere, through a central plenum to the intake runners and eventually to the heads. The design of the manifold can have a great affect on the horsepower and torque curves.

If the vehicle is intended for street use the dual plane manifold is the one to use. This manifold design offers good low end torque and will offer good air flow throughout the RPM band normally associated with street use...idle to 5500 RPM.

linkage, bell-cranks, and adjustments, this system is ideal. Not only are these systems impractical for street use but today there are manifold systems that are superior in performance for racing use.

What, exactly is an intake manifold? The term manifold means multiple or "many fold." The manifold gathers air at a source common to all cylinders, immediately after the throttle air control valves, and distributes it to all the cylinders. The design of the manifold can have a great effect on horsepower and torque curves.

I think that it is time that we discuss what performance is. Performance is making the engine most efficiently accomplish its designated mission. Although it may ruffle the feathers of those that have Hurst tattooed on their palms, even a stock 40hp Volkswagen 1200 can be a performance engine under this definition. A common mistake that is made by the typical performance modifier is a failure to decide exactly the intended purpose of the engine.

Which category is your intended result?
• Fuel economy
• Towing or hauling capacity
• Streetable horsepower
• Horsepower for the track only
We will begin by discussing manifold designs used with cen-

tralized air/fuel mixing systems. There are basically two types of fuel systems that qualify as centralized air/fuel mixing systems-carburetors and throttle body injection. Intake manifolds for these fuel systems come in many different designs. Each of these designs takes advantage of the

100mi tall column of air in a different way.

## Parts of the manifold
### Central plenum
### Dual Plane Plenum

The area of the intake manifold that is common to all the cylinders is called the central

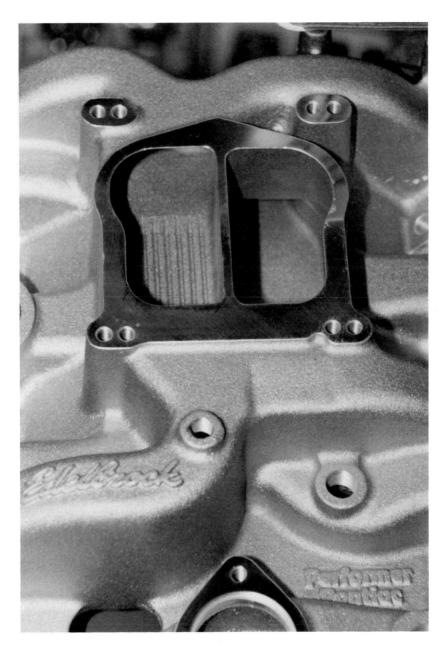

If the vehicle is intended for street use the dual plane manifold is the one to use. This manifold design offers good low end torque and will offer good air flow throughout the RPM band normally associated with street use...idle to 5500 RPM.

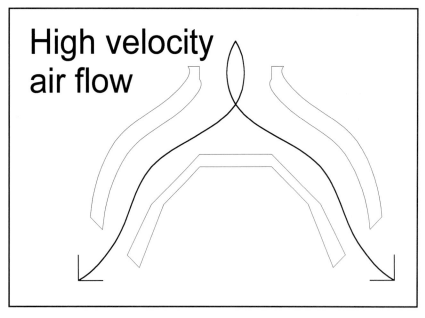

# High velocity air flow

Single plenum manifolds used with throttle body injection systems have performance characteristics very much like a carburetor. The vacuum requirements of a throttle body injection system are not as great as for the carburetor. A throttle body injection system uses the force of fuel pressure above atmospheric to mix the fuel with the air. A carburetor requires a reduced vacuum in the venturi to draw the fuel into the air stream. The result of using a carburetor on a single plane manifold is usually a poor mix of air and fuel at low speeds. Since the TBI system uses positive pressure on the fuel to create this mix a TBI system mounted on a single plane manifold will gain the benefits enjoyed by the carburetor at high engine speeds without as significant a loss of smooth performance at low engine speeds.

plenum. This central plenum has two basic forms—single plane and dual plane. Now the question comes to mind, "Which of these is better?" That question begs the question, "How are you going to use the engine?" The dual plane manifold is best suited for such applications as retrieving the family groceries and towing the boat to the lake. The dual plane manifold offers superior low end torque.

When shopping the catalogs, the enthusiast will notice that the little ads below the pictures in the catalog often offer rpm bands of featured performance. The dual plane manifolds are usually designed for operation between idle and 5500rpm. This, of course, means that most applications rolling of the assembly line to take ma and pa to the feed store use dual plane manifold designs.

Performance applications where the dual plane manifold is most suitable include those where low end torque and smooth transition from idle to power is important. These manifolds depend on engine vacuum to fill the cylinders on the intake stroke. Engines equipped with camshafts and valve timing that provide high engine vacuum at low engine speed are ideal candidates for this type of manifold. The limitation of the dual plane manifold is that at higher engine speeds the vacuum created by the pistons begins to drop off. As the vacuum drops the pressure differential between the atmosphere and the cylinder on the intake stroke begins to drop.

As this pressure differential decreases airflow begins to drop off, as the air flow drops off engine speed will drop, as the engine speed drops the pressure differential will increase, as the pressure differential increases, air flow will increase, as the air flow increases the engine speed will increase. This cycle will repeat itself indefinitely. Of course if the speed at which this will occur is higher than the maximum speed at which the pistons and connecting rods will hold together, and the maximum speed at which the valve springs can adequately close the valves, then the dual plane manifold will be adequate. The result is that the dual plane intake manifold provides good airflow, torque and power when the manifold vacuum is high, but this ability begins to taper off at higher engine speeds.

## Single Plane Plenum

The single plane manifold is used on applications that are intended for pure power. In these intake manifolds the air has a straight path from the bottom of the carburetor to the top of the intake valves. These manifolds provide incredible potential airflow at high speeds. However, life and the laws of physics have a way of making life complicated. While good at providing exceptional airflow when the engine is at high speeds, they provide lousy performance when the engine is running at a low speed.

Now if you are living in Phoenix, Arizona, this could come in handy. Decades ago the streets in that town were laid out in a grid of one mile squares. Over the years streets have popped up on and in between the one mile grid lines. In most parts of town where a mountain does not make it impossible there is a cross-street

Single plane manifolds are designed to ensure maximum velocity of the combustion chamber. This means that these manifolds are at their best at high engine speed when the intake vacuum is always at its lowest.

The point is that a single plane manifold is preferable to the dual plane manifold for the track, but not suitable for the torque, horsepower and rpm curves required for that trip to the 7-Eleven.

Now, in the ideal world a higher being would have created a manifold that was both dual plane and single plane in character. There are many intake manifolds on the market that are designed to be a good compromise between the dual plane and the single plane. There are even several stock applications that literally have two separate intake manifolds: one for low speed and low end torque and another for high speed and high horsepower. The fuel injection computer switches from one manifold to the other at approximately 2200rpm. Fascinating? Well read on, that system is discussed later.

and a stop light every quarter mile. If you are heading to the local Seven-Eleven and pull up to a stop light on Indian School Road you know that it is exactly a quarter-mile to the next stop light. As the lights on the cross-street turn yellow you rev the engine to four grand the light turns greens you dump the clutch leaving the stop light in a cloud of white tire smoke. As the tach approaches 8000rpm you slam the shifter into second gear the rear end slides slightly to the left on a film of molten rubber the tach hits 8000 again you grab third gear. Moments later you find yourself sitting on the side of the road with one of Phoenix's finest leaning in the window saying "You in a heapa trouble boy." One hundred and eighty five dollars lighter, you have the satisfaction of knowing that you made it from stop light to stop light faster than the last fool.

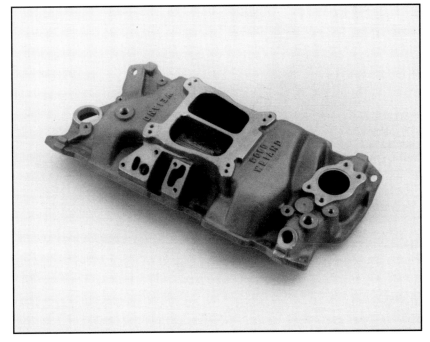

This Weiand manifold is a street legal performance dual plane design. It offers improved performance with streetable driving characteristics. The dual plane manifold depends on engine "vacuum" to flow the air into the cylinders. This makes the manifold work best when the vacuum is at its highest. Vacuum is at its highest when the engine is running at the relatively low engine speeds of street operation.

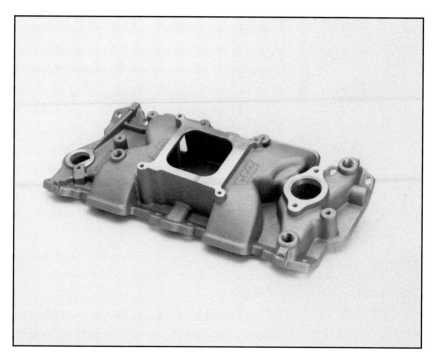

This Weiand single plane manifold depends on air velocity to flow the air into the cylinders. When the throttle is closed the total mass of air entering the engine is small. Therefore the velocity of the air is quite low. At low engine speeds this type manifold does not provide driveability. When the engine speeds are well above idle the volume of the air and therefore the velocity of the air increases. This manifold is powerful for the track but may make trips to the grocery store a bit of an uncomfortable ordeal.

above atmospheric pressure. Imagine throwing a spring through a weightless vacuum. We grab the spring by the end opposite the target and shove it toward the target. When the leading end of the spring hits the target the trailing end will continue to travel until it also hits the target or until the amount of energy required to further compress the spring equalizes with the energy stored in the compressed portion of the spring. The high velocity air traveling through the manifold will do the same thing. The greater the air velocity the greater the energy in the moving air mass. This means that it will require that a greater pressure in the cylinder be required to halt the air flow. As a result the cylinder may be charged to a pressure greater than atmospheric, or "supercharged."

## Compromise Manifolds

The are many street performance manifolds on the market that attempt to give the enthusi-

Where the dual plane manifold depends on engine vacuum to ensure that the cylinder is filled with air when the intake valve opens and the piston moves down on the intake manifold, the single plane manifold depends on air velocity. This type of manifold is particularly suited for applications where the camshaft design and valve timing allow very little intake vacuum. These engines notoriously idle very poorly and have erratic or poor low speed engine operation. The straight-through design of these intake manifolds does not enhance the ability of the engines to create intake manifold vacuum. In fact, they capitalize on the low vacuum characteristics by permitting maximum air velocity. The velocity of the air helps to ensure the filling of the cylinder and can even "force-feed" the cylinder to

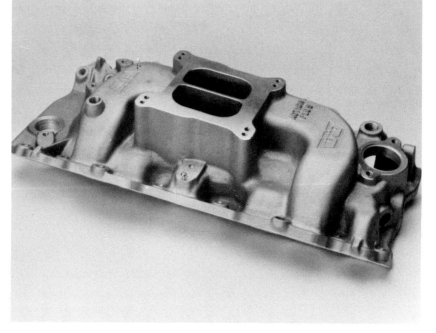

A manifold of this general design may provide an adequate compromise. Although dual plane in design, it is also high rise. A compromise between velocity and vacuum.

The Ford 3.0 SHO multipoint fuel injected engine takes advantage of the fuel source being located near the intake valves. This design makes it possible to use variable length runners. At low engine speeds the engine uses the long manifold runners to maximize vacuum for maximum air flow. At about 2200 RPM the computer signals the manifold to switch from the long high vacuum runners to the short high velocity runners.

ast a little of the best of both worlds. These are typically high rise dual plane manifolds—the throttle body or carburetor mount is located high above the intake valves.

## Legal Replacement Manifolds

The intake manifold is an integral part of the emission control system. Replacing the intake manifold amounts to a fundamental intrusion into the integrity of the emission control system. For this reason there are very few 50 state street legal intake manifold replacements. According to the California Air Resources Board bulletin Reference No. A-92-443 there is only one approved replacement manifold that is legal in California, the strictest of all states. This legal replacement is made by Weiand Automotive Industries. The "Intake Manifold Model 8000" is a legal replacement for carbureted small-block engines ranging from the 283 to the 400cid. Included engines are the Chevy 283, 302, 305, 307, 327, 350, or 400ci engines. The CARB (California Air Resources Board) reference number for this D-256 dated May 21, 1992.

## Spider, 360 degree manifolds

There is nothing to prevent this design from being street legal except the dedication of the manifold manufacturer to make it so. To be 49 state legal it is required that all the original emission devices are provided for on the intake manifold. To be 50 state legal the manifold must be approved for your specific application by the California Air Resources Board. If you select a 360 degree manifold for street use be sure that it is legal in your jurisdiction before handing over the credit card. These manifolds are designed for high speed opera-

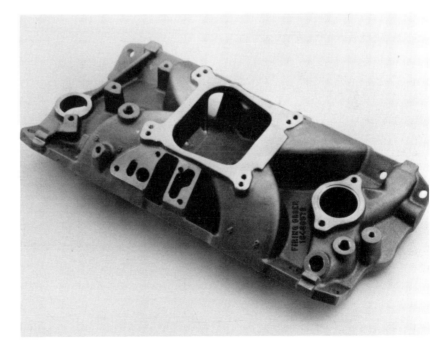

This manifold shows the scars of a performance product designed to meet emission requirements. There are places for choke spring heaters, for EGR valves and an assortment of temperature sensors and thermal vacuum switches.

The 360 degrees manifold is best suited for a car that will never see the white stripe of anything other than the track. While fantasies of commuting in a fire breathing street rod might seem nice, the reality of the stop and go nature of metropolitan traffic precludes the reasonable possibility.

tion. The path for the air is as straight as possible from the carburetor to the intake valve. The 360degree manifold has excellent power characteristics at high speeds but provides very poor idling characteristics.

Keep in mind that new replacement approvals are issued frequently. If a manufacturer advertises its product is 50 state legal it is relatively safe to assume that it is.

## Intake runners

The manifold runners extend from the central plenum to the intake ports on the head. The straighter the airflow path through these runners, the greater the airflow velocity, all other things being equal. Single plane intake manifolds have very straight manifold runners. Dual plane manifolds will have a few twists and turns in the runners. Compromise manifolds are usually dual plane with relatively straight runners.

## Manifold height

How high the throttle plates sit above the intake valve can have a great effect on the performance characteristics of the intake manifold. For carbureted and central point fuel injection applications, the height of the manifold directly affects the angle of airflow between the throttle plates and the intake valve. The higher the manifold, the straighter the path from the throttle plates to the intake valve. This seems like an easy problem to resolve. We will design the intake manifold to place the throttle about five feet above the intake valve. The problem with this is that the fuel is carried with the air. These long manifold runners would give the fuel time to drop out of suspension. This is not a problem for multi-point fuel injected engines. In these systems the fuel is not introduced into the air stream until the air is just above the intake valve. As we will discuss later, this allows for a great deal more flexibility than there is with the central fuel injection systems.

## Runner length

Runner length and throttle plate height are directly related. On the centralized air/fuel mixing systems, the runner length is a compromise between the need for

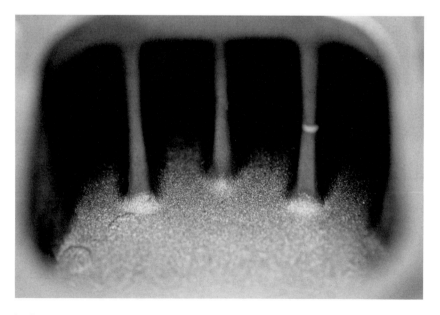

In the 360 degrees manifold the pathways to the intake valves form a circle around the central plenum area. The path to the intake valve is straight and easy. As long as the air velocity is high this works very well but when the engine is asked to idle and intake velocities decrease these low vacuum manifolds do not perform very well.

The runners of this manifold lead in a straight line from the central plenum area to the cylinder head intake ports.

This design maximizes the velocity of the air at high engine speeds.

engine torque and the need to keep the air/fuel charge mixed in the intake manifold. Up to a point the longer the intake runners, the greater the low end torque. However, with increased runner length the engine sacrifices both maximum horsepower output and air/fuel charge uniformity. The shorter the intake runner, up to a point, the greater the maximum power, the greater the uniformity of the air/fuel charge, but the less the maximum torque at low engine speeds. In the ideal universe there would be a manifold that would have long runners at low engine speeds and they would shorten as the engine speed increases. This would be very awkward to do on a centralized air/fuel mixing system; however, several

automobile manufacturers are putting the technology to work on multipoint fuel injected engines.

## Cross-ram induction

In the sixties the "big-iron" manufacturers were doing all in their power to beat one another at the ability to throw the consuming public's head into the back seat when leaving a stoplight. They were trying to beat one another at the ability to leave voluminous clouds of white smoke at every stop sign. At the same time they were trying to imitate the ever lowering silhouettes of the race cars of the time. Putting a high rise manifold on an engine meant placing the hood higher and raising the silhouette. The solution? Cross-ram

induction. This manifold design places the central plenum feeding the right bank of the engine over the left valve cover, and the plenum feeding the left bank of the engine over the right valve cover. The result was long intake runners, a low silhouette, and valve cover gaskets the replacement of which made thousands of chiropractors extremely wealthy.

## Stock manifolds

The perfect intake for a carbureted or TBI-equipped engine would be one with long runners for good bottom end torque, but with short runners for good performance at high speeds. The short runners would also be prevent the fuel from falling out of the air/fuel mixture. The long

As teenagers my peers and I always had the greatest respect for anyone that had installed a "high-rise" manifold on their car. We did not know why we had this respect, we just did. The higher the manifold, the more direct the path to the intake valve.

Therefore, especially at high engine speeds, the greater the velocity of the air. When the velocity is sufficiently high it will "cram" itself into the cylinder. These manifolds, however, do not provide for smooth operation at low speeds and idle.

runners would provide for maximum air velocity, ensuring the cylinders would be filled with air/fuel charge each time the intake valve opens. Short manifold runners provide for smooth operation at low engine speeds. The fuel remains evenly mixed with the air in the intake system as it is transported to the combustion chamber. Since most street applications are driven by those less interested in performance than getting to the job site in comfort engineers will usually choose the smoothness of operation that is

associated with the short runner intake manifold.

## "High rise" manifolds

Those of us who grew up in the sixties fall into two categories—the ones who drove around in red VW microbuses looking for places to dump their garbage, as per Arlo Guthrie, and those of us whose hands automatically conform to the shape of a Hurst shifter "furry T-handle." It takes those of us in the latter category to truly appreciate the long runner manifold. When the throt-

tle plates of the carburetor open, a long low pressure area is created in the manifold. The 100mi column of air then tries to force its

Next page: In the ideal universe intake manifolds would be able to change their length as the engine operating conditions change. They would be long at low engine speeds when torque was needed and be short at high engine speeds when horsepower was needed. This technology has been developed and is used by several manufacturers on multipoint fuel injection systems.

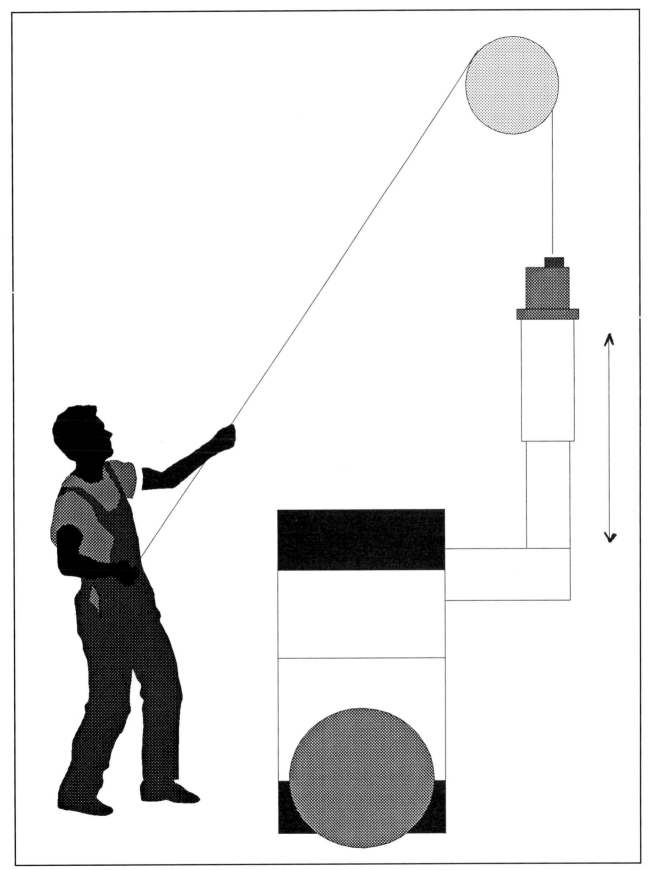

This B&M blower equipped engine illustrates the concept of cross-ram induction very well. Although mounted on a blower notice that the left carburetor feeds the right side of the engine and the right carburetor feeds the left side of the engine. The stock versions of this concept were often difficult to work around.

way into the cylinder. As the air travels through long intake manifold runners its velocity will tend to decrease. The goal of a high rise manifold is to make the trip from the carburetor or throttle body unit as short, straight and direct as possible. The short direct path with keep the velocity as high as possible.

The effect is similar to that of air moving through a wind tunnel. The result is a rush of air toward the combustion chamber, a rush of air with sufficient velocity to insure that the cylinder will be filled to as close to atmospheric pressure as possible and hopefully beyond. That rush of air will be translated into a half a pound of rubber on the pavement.

The inertia of the air flowing through the intake causes it to behave like the toy trains in the sixties TV comedy *The Addam's Family*. In that show the characters were hooked on playing with toy trains, not like most kids on Christmas morning (or really dads on Christmas Eve), but

rather staging train wrecks. When the locomotive collided with a stationary object and stopped, the caboose wanted to keep traveling. The result was an accordion-like pile up with the caboose nearly as close to the stationary object as the locomotive. In the "high rise" manifold the air travels like the train. When the lead part of the air column comes in contact with a stationary object, in the form of the piston and exhaust valve, the trailing part of the air presses on like the caboose of the train. The end result is a supercharging effect. At some engine speeds the effect can raise the volumetric efficiency of the cylinder above 100 percent.

So far the "high rise" manifold sounds good. The problem is that as the engine speed increases a resonance may be set up in the manifold. These resonances can impede air flow in much the same way a bobsled will be slowed as it travels down the run and bounces off the walls.

Remember that the air does not flow steadily into the intake system. The opening of an intake valve in the engine and the corresponding dropping of the piston in the cylinder causes a rapid increase in airflow. As the various intake valves open and close the airflow rate in the intake fluctuates. The fluctuations create pressure pulsations in the intake manifold that contribute to the resonances.

I suppose you are thinking by now: "Well if I buy a manifold off the shelf for high performance use, it should improve the performance of my engine." Unfortunately, no such assumption can be made. Any reader that has also read my book on cylinder heads or engine rebuilding knows that I am a definite advocate of the flow bench. While it is not a perfect instrument for determining airflow it is better than a guess. In the ideal world—say the Borelian colony of Betazar Four near the inner part of the Sol spiral of the Milky Way—you would be able to test all the camshafts, lifters, rocker arms, cylinder heads, throttle bores (or carburetors), and intake manifolds on a flow test bench. This would be the only accurate way to test your combination. Each of the components can affect each other. Resonances that inhibit airflow can occur in the manifold with one carburetor or cylinder head and yet that same manifold can flow perfectly with another combination.

This is not the ideal world (and, in fact, neither is the Borelian colony of Betazar Four near the inner part of the Sol spiral of the Milky Way). When you decide on the manifold that is right for your combination the best bet is to seek out someone who has successfully used that combination before. Imitating is the best route toward success. But more about selection later.

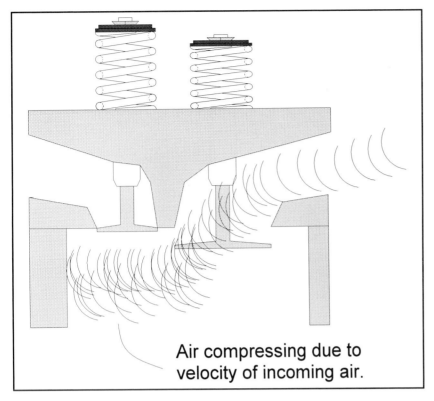

## Air compressing due to velocity of incoming air.

When the air flows through an intake system that has long intake runners it gathers velocity. This velocity is carried into the combustion chamber where it serves to "supercharge" the cylinder. At certain engine speeds and load conditions this effect can increase the volumetric efficiency above 100 percent.

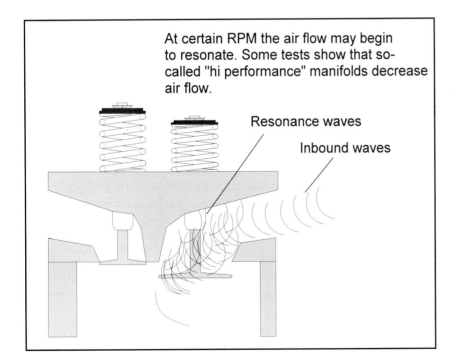

At certain RPM the air flow may begin to resonate. Some tests show that so-called "hi performance" manifolds decrease air flow.

Resonance waves

Inbound waves

### When the air hits the floor

You may have been walking around your local performance shop during the past few weeks and noticed "spacers" hanging on pegboards along the walls. When air flows into the central plenum area of a carburetor manifold it must turn a corner and head down the runner to the intake valve. The pressure pulses that have been previously discussed come at regular intervals. In the time between each of the pulses the air mass will flow a distance that is proportional to the velocity of that mass. As the speed of the engine changes the velocity of that air mass will change, as the velocity of the air mass changes the distance between the pressure pulses changes. The smooth-est flow to the combustion chamber will occur if the distance between the pressure pulse is exactly equal to the distance from the carburetor to the floor of the manifold central plenum. The result is that the best air flow will only occur at certain engine speeds. The spacers help to "tune" the manifold for best air flow.

When the air mass pulse crashes against the floor of the manifold several things happen. First, the loss of momentum causes some of the fuel to be left behind rather than being carried to the cylinder. This leans the air/fuel ratio. The leaner mixture will provide less heat energy to expand the air in the cylinder. Less heat energy, less power.

There is an air flow rate where virtually every intake manifold will set up resonance waves. The trick that the manifold designer has to pull off is keep the resonance to a minimum within the RPM band for which the manifold is being designed. They do not always succeed. Often the expensive "high performance" manifold will decrease the performance of the engine rather than increase.

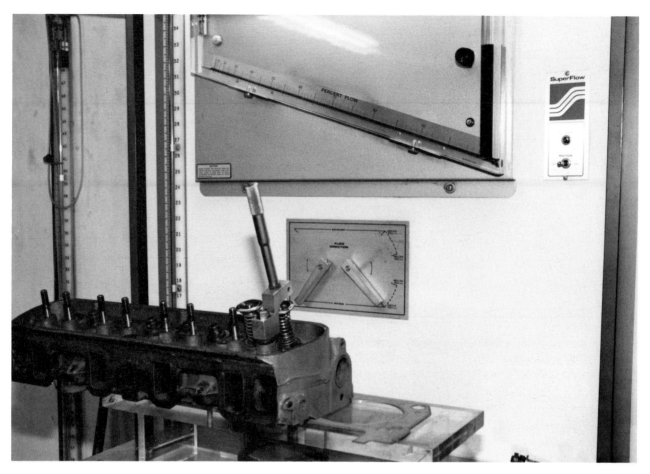

Although generally used just for cylinder head air flow measurements a flow bench can also be used to find the best intake manifold for your needs. Decide your peak power RPM, your camshaft and valve lift, then try an assortment of manifolds to find the one that provides the best flow.

The second result of the crash of the air mass against the floor is a loss in the momentum of that air mass. This loss in momentum is a lot like the loss of momentum experienced by the twin-engine Beachcraft as it crashed through the tissue paper billboard in Stanley Kramer's *Mad, Mad, Mad World*.

If the purpose of the engine is to take mom and pop to the mall, or to impress a pubescent colleague, then this floor crashing makes little difference. But if trimming a few fractions of a second off the ET is the goal then it is of critical importance. Adding spacers to reduce crashing is not

a simple matter. Many things must be taken into consideration. What is the rpm targeted for maximum power and airflow? How many cylinders does the engine have? What is the wave length of the air pulses? To know the wavelength of the air pulses, it is necessary to know the velocity of the airflow. To find the velocity of the airflow, it is necessary to know the length and diameter of the manifold from the throttle bore to the top of the piston. This is a complex science which will ultimately become an art of trial and error. Let us discuss a formula to use for a starting point.

Example: An eight cylinder engine with a nominal RPM of 5000 will create 20,000 air pressure pulses per minute. This amount to 333.33 pressure pulses per second. If there was no manifold and the cylinder head were to dematerialize on the intake stroke the distance between the pressure pulses would be totally dependent on stroke, the number of cylinders and RPM.

Let us say that we have a have an eight cylinder engine with a 3 inch stroke and a 4 inch bore. This would make the engine a 302 (sorry Chevy fans). At 5000 RPM each cylinder will inhale 54.6 cubic feet of air each

This assortment of spacers is typical of those used to tune the manifold for maximum air flow. Selection of the proper height spacer can be done by trial and error, by advice from those who have built engine and manifold combinations similar to yours, and by the use of a flow bench.

$$CID = pi/4 * (bore * bore) * stroke * no. of cylinders$$

This is the formula for calculating the cubic inches of displacement when the bore, stroke and number of cylinders is known.

minute. On each stroke the piston will pull a column of air 3 inches long. The 4 inch bore of the cylinder will have a cross-section of 12.6 square inches. When we add an intake manifold and cylinder head we will find that their cross-section will be significantly smaller than the cross-section of the cylinder. It will often be rectangular in shape. If the narrowest dimension of the air flow path is 1.5 inches by 2 inches the cross-section will be 3 square inches. The cylinder bore cross-section is over 4 times larger than the cross-section of the intake air flow path. This means that if we are to fill the cylinder to 100 percent atmospheric pressure we will have to force an air mass approximately 3 inches long and 4 inches in diameter (equal to bore and stroke) through a passageway only 1.5 by 2 inches. This is not be a problem if the time allowed to move the air in the cylinder is long. At slow engine speeds, therefore, there is little problem. In effect the narrowest part of the air intake system can massage the air into a long thin string, like a pair of hands rolling clay back and forth, then reform the air into a short wide mass in the cylinder. As the engine speed increases the time allowed to perform this bit of art decreases. The decrease in time is due to the shortening time interval between the opening and closing of the intake valve. If the speed of the engine increases to the point where the intake valve closes before the long string of air mass can move into the cylinder and form into the 4x3 inch mass then the cylinder will not be filled to atmospheric pressure. If maximum power is to be achieved it is necessary to fill the cylinder to full atmospheric pressure. Any percent short of atmospheric pressure will result in a corresponding shortness in power.

All of the above assumes that the throttle plates are in the wide open position. It becomes quickly irrelevant as the throttle opening decreases as the throttle closes. When the throttle is not wide open the limiting factor in filling the cylinder to 100 percent of atmospheric pressure is the throttle plate, no longer the intake manifold or cylinder head.

## Selecting an intake manifold for carburetion

How do you select the proper manifold for your use? First of all you need to honestly assess how the engine is to be used. While it might be nice to dream of taking your 305 Chevy Caprice to the Winternationals, it is hardly likely that you will. While it might be nice to dream of driving your 600hp Camaro to the office there are two realities to consider. First, stop and go traffic in metropolitan

There is little thoroughly satifying about spending a great deal of money on a compromise manifold. The engine will not run smoothly at low engine speeds and the increase in power will either be mostly psychological or a disappointment.

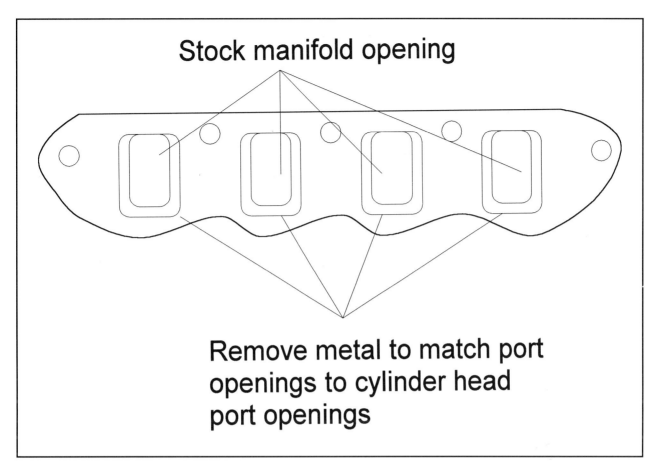

Stock manifold opening

Remove metal to match port openings to cylinder head port openings

I have always been fascinated by the unusual performance car. Many years before I was gray in the beard I admired a member of the local sports car club who had spiced up a "stock" mid-sixtes Morris Minor. Anyone can buy off-the-shelf parts to make a 350 Chevy howl, the fun is in improving the performance of an engine when off-the-shelf performance products are not available.

areas makes it difficult to keep the engine speed high enough to ensure good airflow through some manifolds. Secondly, if you are fortunate enough to live in a rural area, and if you are not at least a third cousin of the county sheriff, you might find yourself collecting enough traffic tickets to make even David Letterman envious. Although compromise manifolds do allow for some flexibility in this decision, the reality here is that the compromise manifold is like taking your sister to the prom: none of your desires will be fully satisfied.

After deciding track, street or compromise, the next thing to determine is the rpm range of the engine. For consumer convenience most manifold manufacturers describe their manifolds in catalogs by the rpm range in which they will be used. This needs to be an honest assessment of the actual range of operation. If you live in Santa Fe Springs, California, and work in Long Beach from 8:00 a.m.-5:00 p.m., it is unlikely that any commuter rig will be run in the 4000-8000rpm range, even if you do have a "granny low." On the other hand, if you are running 4.11:1 or lower gears, you live in North Platte, Nebraska, and work in Ogallala, your brother is the county sheriff and your work hours are different from everyone else in Nebraska, then it might make some sense for you to use a high rise 360degree manifold. And of course if the engine has been built exclusively for track use a high rise 360degree manifold is a given.

**Improving the existing manifold**

In most cases you are far better off to replace the existing manifold rather than try to improve it. However, we live in a world where emission control laws dictate what we can and cannot do to our engines. What this means to the world of high performance equipment is that only engines that a performance equipment manufacturer believes will have a large market share outside of California will have performance manifolds built for it. The older the car is, the easier it is to meet emission requirements for performance equipment. What all this means on the bottom line is that older engines and engine designs have a great deal of performance equipment available for them, while newer engine and engine designs do not. This means that just like the early drag-racers, those daring men and women who stepped forth from the primordial ooze of the mundane automobile we too the performance minded individuals of the nineties are forced to use machining and grinding skills to improve the existing manifold.

Many of the key principles of machining the manifold are the same as the principles of machining the cylinder head especially since the needs of the head and combustion chamber dictate the design of the intake manifold. Let us take a look.

## The proper tools

A high-speed grinder and a carbide grinding bit are needed for porting the intake manifold. These are quite expensive (do not expect to find such a tip on the bargain table at the local hardware store), but quite durable. You will need a second, finer bit for polishing the ports.

## Porting

This operation involves the reshaping of the intake runners to improve airflow. When the intake was designed by the manufacturer a great deal of attention was given to port design and airflow. Then, depending on the manufacturer, a degree of compromise was given to requirements for mass production. As a result there are many imperfections in the design and execution of each intake. A noteworthy exception is the previously mentioned GM Tuned Port manifold. The goal of porting the manifold

is to ensure that the potential flow rate through the intake is greater than the theoretical flow rate past the open valve at maximum valve lift. Further, to ensure maximum and balanced airflow, the volumes of the intake runners must be equal.

The airflow rate when the valve is at maximum valve opening is represented by the surface area of the imaginary cylinder formed between the top edge of the valve margin and the bottom edge of the valve seat. If the maximum valve lift is 0.5in and the valve diameter is 2in then a cylinder 0.5in tall and 2in in diameter is formed. The formula to convert these measurements to a surface area is shown in these two examples:

$$\Pi \cdot \text{Diameter} \cdot \text{Lift}$$
$$3.14 \cdot 2 \cdot 0.5 = \text{Square inches}$$

The significance of this is that if we have a straight path for the air to follow, and if the width of the intake runner is 1.25in at its narrowest point, the height must at no point be less than 2.09in.

$$\frac{\text{Open Valve Area}}{\text{Width}} = \text{Minimum Height}$$

Any point that is smaller will create a restriction greater than the valve. This formula assumes a straight flow of the air through the head. There are very few heads, other than those designed specifically for racing engines, that have straight ports.

## Resizing the ports

Use the carbide grinder to open the intake runner port to match the intake manifold gasket and intake port of the cylinder head. If you need to enlarge the port, and there are many intakes which will not require port enlargement, emphasize enlargement of the top—make the top of the port higher and wider.

## Checking with silicone goop

Now it is time to check your work. Chicago Latex and Permaflex Mould Company both make a latex compound that is used to check the relative size and shape of the ports. Spray all the surfaces of the intake runners with WD-40 or similar lubricant. Slant the manifold slightly so that one end of the manifold is slightly above the other. Tilting the intake reduces the possibility of bubbles being trapped in the latex when it is poured into the runner. Mix the latex according to the instructions provided, and fill the intake runner with the compound. Pour slowly to reduce the possibility of an air bubble being trapped. Repeat this process for the other cylinders.

Once the latex is set, carefully remove the molds along with the valves. When they are all out you will have a 3-D representation of the runners. Now retouch the runners to match your first "model" runner.

## Polishing

A high luster "spit shine" is not what is referred to when we mention polishing the ports. In fact, it has been shown in many industries that when a surface is too polished it can impede rather than help fluid flow. Also, if the surface is slightly rough it creates turbulence that helps keep the fuel suspended in the flowing air. When you polish the runners you are looking for casting ridges and places where the walls of the port become abruptly rougher than the rest of the runner. Ridges and sudden increases in the roughness of the surface can decrease airflow through the intake.

Using the grinder motor that was used to port the intake and a grinding bit that is finer than the one used to re-size the intake port, remove the casting ridges and smooth out any steps and grooves, to allow good flow.

# Chapter 4
## Components of Electronic
## Fuel Injection Systems

The problems associated with maximizing air flow and keeping the fuel mixed with the air are problems shared by both carburetor and throttle body injection (TBI) systems. One of the main advantages of TBI systems over carburetors is that the carburetor can be a serious restriction to air flow. In order to measure air flowing through the carburetor most employ a venturi. The venturi causes a pressure drop in the air mass flowing through it that allows atmospheric pressure to push fuel from the fuel bowl into the intake air stream. Fuel injection systems have no such venturi and therefore no such restriction to air flow. However, fuel injection systems do need to measure air flow. Some of the methods of measuring air flow in fuel injection systems create a restriction to air flow, some do not.

### Air measuring devices
### Manifold absolute pressure sensor (MAP sensor)

All domestic throttle body injection systems use a MAP sensor to measure air flow. Many import applications also use MAP sensors to measure air flow. Many port fuel injection systems also use MAP sensors.

Ford used them almost exclusively on their port fuel injection applications throughout the eighties, Chrysler continues to use it on all its non-Mitsubishi applications.

The MAP sensor senses airflow by measuring the difference between barometric and manifold pressure. When the engine is being started the computer senses the manifold pressure as the key is rotated through the "on" position heading toward "start." This sample of barometric pressure is stored in a memory and referred to by the computer until the engine is turned off. The pressure in the manifold begins to vary as the engine runs; the closer it is to the barometric sample, the greater the load the engine is under.

Before going any further with this explanation it should be noted that most technicians and car hobbyists are used to thinking in terms of manifold *vacuum*. The scientific fact is that there has never been a vacuum in the intake manifold. What is in the manifold is a pressure that is lower than atmospheric pressure. We are also used to thinking that when the throttle is opened the manifold vacuum decreases; the reality of this is that the manifold pressure is increasing, and because the pressure is increasing, the reading on a vacuum gauge drops.

### GM and Chrysler Manifold Pressure Sensors

The MAP Sensor consists of an extremely thin diaphragm strung between four variable resistors that form a "Wheatstone Bridge." When the pressure on the diaphragm increas-

The most important fuel injection sensor to think about when you are considering a manifold replacement is the manifold pressure sensor. In a very real sense the MAP sensor replaces the venturi function of the carburetor. If the MAP sensor is physically relocated too far away from the manifold a lag in acceleration may occur. Although a multipoint fuel injected engine notice that the MAP sensor of this Quad 4 is mounted between the two center runners of the intake manifold. The proximity of the MAP sensor to the central plenum of the manifold ensures a minimum lag in performance.

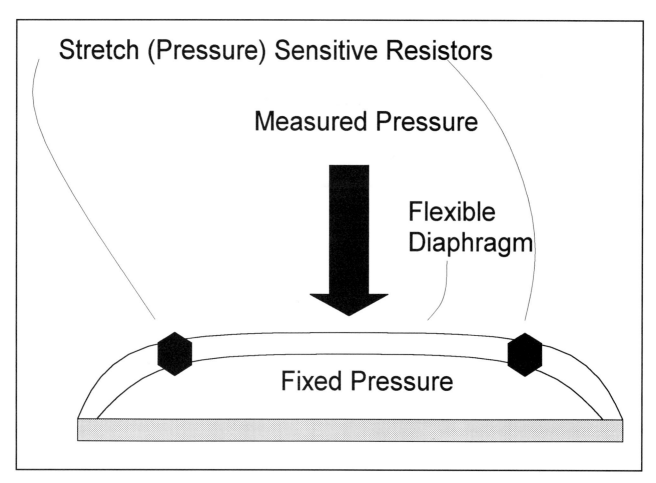

## Stretch (Pressure) Sensitive Resistors

Measured Pressure

Flexible Diaphragm

Fixed Pressure

Back in the days when Andy lived in Mayberry you would bolt on a performance manifold, bolt on a carburetor and you would be ready to go to the drag strip. Today when planning a performance car you may be dealing with

a fuel injection system, you may be dealing with emission laws. Fuel injection systems must be able to accurately measure air flow. One of the more popular ways to do this is with a variable voltage manifold absolute pres-

sure (MAP) sensor. The most common MAP sensor, which is used by both GM and Chrysler, produces a variable voltage by using a silicone diaphram to stretch variable resistors.

es the resistors are stretched causing their resistance to change. The result is the output voltage of the sensor varies from reference voltage as the pressure on the diaphragm changes. For most applications using this type of sensor full atmospheric pressure causes an output voltage of about 4.5 volts (where reference voltage is 5 volts). At or near sea level an idling engine will cause the voltage signal from the MAP sensor to be between 1.2 and 1.9 volts, usually averaging about 1.5. (These voltages are approximate.) This drop in voltage is proportional to the

drop in manifold pressure that occurs when the engine is at an idle.

Explanation:

**Normal Barometric Pressure**
= 29.9in mercury
= 15psi
= 100kPa
**Variable voltage MAP output**
= 4.5 volts

**Manifold pressure at an idle**
= 10in mercury
= 5psi
= 35kPa

Note that these pressures are about one third of atmospheric.

**MAP sensor output voltage**
= 1.5 volts

### Ford Manifold Pressure Sensors

On Ford applications the MAP sensor produces a variable frequency, rather than a variable voltage. The Ford EEC IV MAP sensor produces a square wave with a frequency that ranges from about 90 to 170 Hertz. Key-on-engine-off, the pressure in the intake manifold is atmospheric, and the MAP sensor output fre-

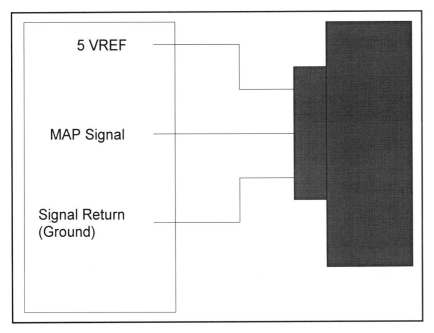

When you decide to make intake modifications on a modern electronically controlled carburetor or fuel injection engine there is a lot more to consider than on an old 409. When intake systems are modified on a modern engine the electronic sensors that monitor the operation of the engine can be affected. One of the most important of these sensors is the manifold pressure sensor. This sensor helps the computer determine intake air flow. Since the changes in intake manifold pressure do not necessarily reflect changes in air flow the performance can be adversely instead of positively affected.

quency is around 160 Hertz. This reading may differ a little depending on altitude and weather conditions. When the engine is started and the intake manifold pressure drops, so does the MAP output frequency. At an idle, the output frequency is usually between 110 and 120 Hertz; on deceleration it drops into the nineties.

As long as the idle voltage, or frequency is in this neighborhood and the voltage increases as the engine load increases (such as when you snap the throttle) and decreases as the engine load decreases then the MAP sensor is functioning normally.

There are three wires connected to the variable frequency sensor. One wire is a five volt power supply to the sensor, a second wire carries the pressure sensor signal to the computer and the third wire is a ground.

It should be noted that, on turbo applications, all of the output voltages for a given pressure are cut in half, which would

Ford uses a MAP sensor that produces a variable frequency 5 volt pulse. Regardless of the type of MAP sensor used, it must be located in such a way that any change in air flow is immediately sensed as manifold pressure. Note the length of the original vacuum hose that runs from the MAP sensor to the intake manifold. The hose should be no loger than the original when the manifold is replaced.

Applications equipped a MAP sensor measure intake air flow by measuring the difference between intake manifold pressure and barometric pressure. The closer the manifold pressure is to barometric pressure, the greater the air flow.

This is the location of the manifold pressure sensor on the 1985 Chrysler multipoint fuel injected engines. This computer would be found in the passenger's kick-panel. The vacuum line between manifold pressure sensor and the manifold is several feet long.

When this vacuum line is this long performance on initial acceleration will suffer. In this application performance is a minor concern, in your street machine any effect on performance may negate the effect of any money you spent on a new manifold.

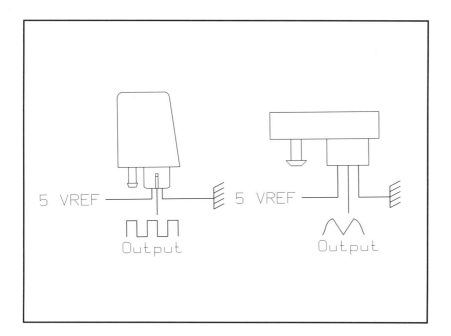

The Ford manifold pressure sensor puts out a different signal from those of GM and Chrysler, however, its proximity to the intke manifold is no less important.

make the idle voltage about .75 volts. This is because the MAP sensor on a turbo not only has to measure pressures below atmospheric but also boost pressures above atmospheric.

## Air flow meter
### Bosch

The Bosch-style airflow meter consists of a spring loaded flap mounted on a rotating shaft. Mounted between the air cleaner and the throttle assembly, all of the air entering the engine passes through it. As the air flows into the engine it moves the flap, which rotates the shaft. The rotating shaft is connected to a variable resistance device known as a potentiometer. As the shaft is rotated, the resistance between the input reference voltage terminal and the output terminal changes; therefore the output voltage changes. A small airflow causes little movement and therefore a small output voltage. A larger airflow causes a greater deflection and therefore a greater output voltage.

A damper flap forms an "L" with the airflow measuring flap. This damper flap reduces the erratic movement of the sensor flap caused by sudden acceleration, deceleration or the normal fluctuations in airflow caused by valve action.

A secondary air channel allows a metered amount of air to bypass the L-shaped flap. Many applications have a manual mixture adjustment screw to control the amount of air allowed through this bypass. If the screw is turned in, it reduces the amount of air allowed through this bypass channel. As a result, more air is forced across the L-shaped flap causing it to be deflected more. The more the L-shaped flap is diverted the greater the output signal to the computer and the more fuel the computer allows through the injectors. As a re-

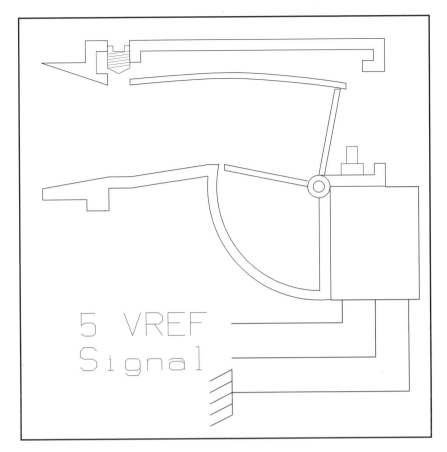

5 VREF
Signal

Left: The Bosch-style air flow meter was introduced in 1974. It has been used by many European and Japanese manufacturers. The airflow meter will remain accurate regardless of the modifications to the engine and intake system up to the point where the airflow excedes the flow rate of the sensor.

sult, the engine runs richer when less air goes through the bypass.

Also included in most airflow meters is a fuel pump switch. When the flap comes to rest indicating that no air is flowing into the engine, the switch opens, shutting off the fuel pump. Most applications also include a thermistor to measure the temperature of incoming air.

Below: The Karman Vortex air flow sensor is used on Mitsubishi applications. This would include applications such as the Dodge Colt that are made by other manufacturers but have Mitsubishi drive trains.

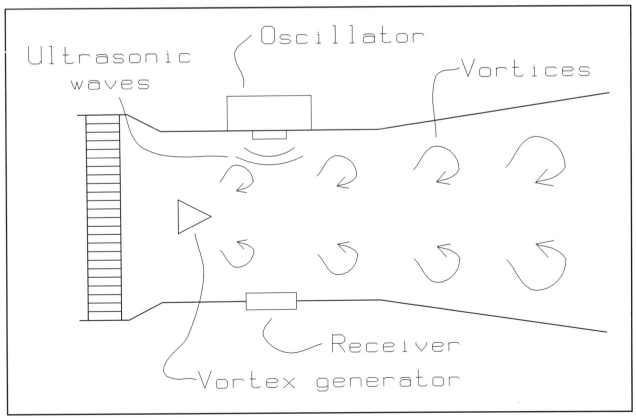

Ultrasonic waves

Oscillator

Vortices

Receiver

Vortex generator

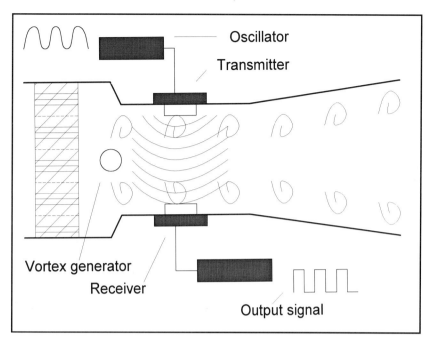

The Karman Vortex sensor is used exclusively on Asian applications, primarily Mitsubishi products. This device is fitted in the air cleaner, very little can be done to improve air flow through the sensor or through the air cleaner.

## Air mass meter
## Bosch

The Bosch air mass meter is located between the air filter and the throttle assembly. All of the air entering the intake system passes through it. The sensor consists of a 0.07 millimeter platinum wire looped across the main channel of airflow. A thermistor in the air mass meter measures the temperature of the incoming air. A "computer" on the side of the sensor passes enough current through the platinum wire to heat it to 100 degrees F above the temperature of the incoming air. As the engine is started and air begins to pass through the intake system, the wire is cooled. The "computer" of the air mass meter notices the drop in resistance that accompanies the cooling of the wire and increases the current flow to maintain the temperature 100 degrees above that of the incom-

## Mitsubishi Karman-vortex

The Karman Vortex sensor is used exclusively on Mitsubishi and Mitsubishi products imported by Chrysler. This sensor is interesting because it hears the mass of air entering the engine. This sensor has a vortex generator across the path of airflow, an ultrasonic generator and an ultrasonic receiver. As air flows through the sensor on its way to the intake manifold it contacts the vortex generator. Vortices are set up. The frequency of these vortices is directly proportional to airflow. The ultrasonic generator emits waves perpendicular to the path of airflow. As these waves meet with the vortices they are accelerated, increasing their frequency in a manner similar to the Doppler effect. The ultrasonic receiver and its associated electronics interprets these frequencies as volumetric airflow and sends a variable frequency square wave to the computer.

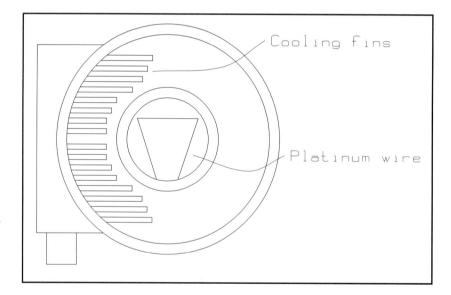

The Bosch Mass Air Flow sensor is used in the LH-Jetronic system popular with many European manufacturers. General Motors chose to use it with the Tuned Port Injection system installed on the 5.0 and 5.7 liter Corvettes, Camaros and Firebirds.

The main sensing element of the Bosch style mass air flow sensor is a platinum wire suspended across the main channel of air flow. While the wire provides very little inhibition to air flow, the tube in which it is mounted is a considerable restriction.

When the engine is shut off the Bosch MAF sensor will heat the platinum wire red hot to clean off any road oil that may have stuck to it while traveling down the road. Note the cooling fins.

ing air. As the sensor varies the current flow through the heated wire, the output voltage of the sensor will also vary from nearly zero to nearly five volts. As the air mass flowing through the sensor increases, the output voltage increases.

Because the air mass meter's platinum wire sits across the main channel of airflow it may become coated by road oils and crankcase vapors. To prevent an "insulating" jacket from being built up over the wire, a "burn-off" cycle is provided. Approximately four seconds after the engine is shut off the ECU grounds a relay which applies power to the platinum wire, heating it red hot. The burn-off lasts for about one second and cleans off anything that may have stuck to the wire while the engine was running.

One of the worst offenders in the restriction of airflow is the Mass Air Flow (MAF) Sensor. The

one used on the Tuned Port Corvette was designed and built by Bosch. One study showed that at a given pressure differential the stock Bosch mass air flow sensor will flow 529 cfm. Keep in mind that the flow rate will change as the pressure differential between the ends of the mass air flow sensor changes. There are screens located at each end of the sensor. These screens were put there to protect the delicate heated wire which is suspended across the main channel of airflow. These same tests show that an increase of 182cfm, up to a very respectable 711cfm, can be obtained by simply removing these screens.

The MAF also has cooling fins for the electronic module on the side of the sensor, which sit across the main channel of airflow. These fins represent a restriction to airflow of about 39cfm. While this is not nearly the restriction created by the screens, these cooling fins repre-

sent a potential loss of about 10 percent of the horsepower potential of the engine. Not only do we have these fins to contend with, but we also have the fact that the hot wire sensing element also sits across the main channel of airflow, seriously reducing the potential airflow. A rough estimate of the restriction created by the sensing element is about 20 percent. We cannot do anything about the sensing element, but we can about the cooling fins.

Legend has it that electronic failures of the MAF occurred during Death Valley testing. These cooling fins were then added to increase the ability of the MAF electronics to give up heat in high temperature environments. There is probably a certain amount of truth to the legend since the "Bosch" fuel injected applications such as Volvo and Porsche sport no such large fins.

If you are not going to be operating the car in a hot weather environment then grab your hacksaw, your two hundred mile an hour tape and get busy. Cover each end of the sensing element venturi (the circle within the circle) with the tape, ensure that the interior of the sensor is free of grease, oil, moisture or anything else which might attract and hold the metal sawdust that is going to result from the removal of the cooling fins, and cut off the fins.

If you are like me you may have something ranging from quiet trepidation to out and out fear about taking a hacksaw to a $400+ electronic component. For people like me TPIS sells a stock unit to replace the one I screw up, or one that is already modified, for less than dealer list. If you prefer and can do without your car for a few days your MAF can be professionally modified for less than $150.

On some applications a potentiometer is located on the side of the sensor. This potentiometer is used to adjust the air fuel ratio.

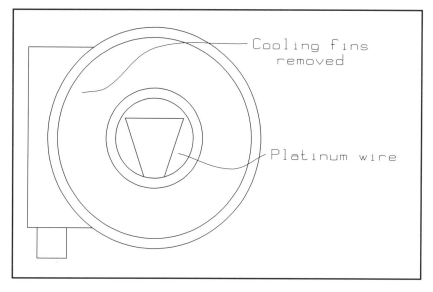

Removing the cooling fins in the Bosch MAF can allow for a considerable increase in air flow. These fins are only needed in the hottest climates. Finless MAFs are available through aftermarket sources such as Tuned Port Injection Specialists.

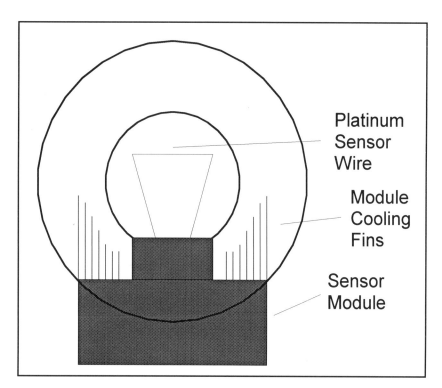

If the car is equipped with the Bosch Mass Air Flow sensor then anything done to the intake system may be limited in effectiveness by the air flow capacity of the MAF. The cooling fins and the venturi around the platinum wire are a restriction to air flow. Removing the cooling fins in relatively mild climates can improve air flow.

The Bosch MAF has five terminals.
  1. 12 volt power supply (or five volt reference)
  2. ground
  3. variable voltage output signal
  4. burn-off 12 volts (voltage here only during burn-off)
  5. burn-off ground

*Delco*
  The Delco MAF works essentially the same way as the Bosch type but there are some important differences. The Delco MAF doesn't use a heated wire to measure the incoming air, instead it uses a piece of Mylar film with a copper conductor in it. The "computer" mounted on the side of the sensor maintains the temperature of the film and converts its control of current through the film into a variable frequency. The frequency varies from 32-150 Hertz, with the lower frequencies indicating a smaller airflow. Also, there is no burn-off.
  Some Delco MAF sensors have three terminals while others have five. For the three wire sensors a 12 volt power supply is connected to one terminal. The second terminal is connected to a ground while the third provides a pulsing ground for a five volt reference from the ECM (computer). As the MAF grounds and ungrounds the ECM's reference signal it creates a variable frequency square wave that varies from 32 to 150 Hertz. As the air flowing through the MAF increases the frequency increases.
  The five wire Delco MAF includes the air temperature input to the computer as well.
  The three wire MAF terminals are:
  1. 12 volt power supply
  2. ground
  3. 32-150 Hertz output
  The five wire MAF terminals are:
  1. 12 volts power supply
  2. ground
  3. 32-150 Hertz output

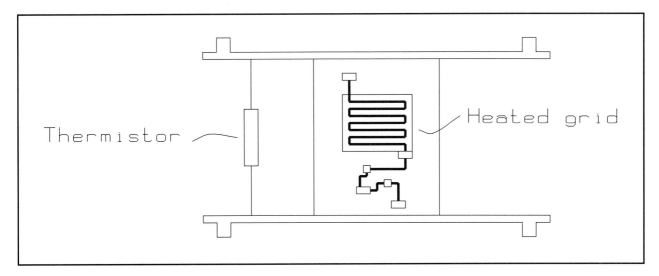

The Delco MAF air flow sensor is a part of American automotive history. This, I suppose, is a polite way of saying that it had such a high failure rate that GM phased it out. The heated grid is the primary air flow sensing component and is also a major restriction to air flow.

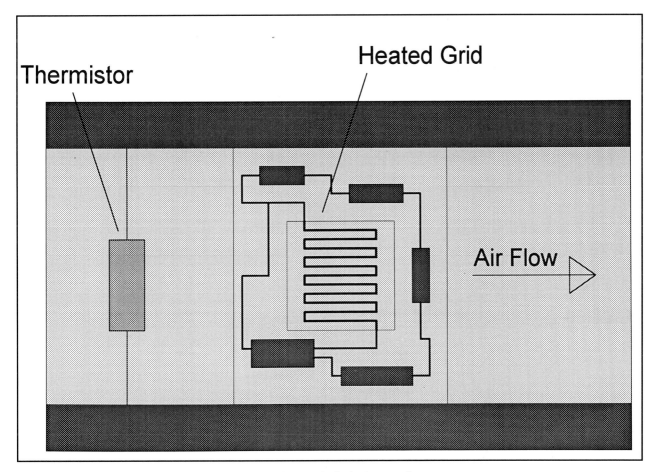

The problem laden Delco mass air flow sensor is a greater restriction to air flow than is the Bosch MAF. Fortunately, its use is limited to applications that are not popular for performance modification.

4. air temperature 5 volt reference

5. ground

The AC/Delco MAF is used only on GM Port Fuel applications, other than the Tuned Port systems. The failure rate on this component seems to be rather high. Symptoms of a defective Delco MAF include stalling and hesitation.

## Hitachi

Hitachi is the source supplier for several manufacturers of a mass airflow sensor which is a heated wire sensor producing either a variable frequency or a variable voltage.

The Hitachi MAF consists of a hollow tube with a bypass channel. The heated wire sensing element sits in this bypass channel, outside the primary path of airflow. This prevents the insulating build-up on the sensing element. Also, since the primary airflow path is unobstructed, there is no restriction to airflow. The ambient temperature reference sensor is also located in this bypass channel.

The Ford applications use a Hitachi style MAF that produces a voltage that ranges from about 0.8 volts at an idle to about 4.0-4.5 volts at wide open throttle and full load. At 60mph the output voltage is around 1.8-2.5 volts.

On GM Applications the Hitachi MAF is similar to the Delco in that it creates a frequency, but the frequency is much higher—more than 1000 Hertz. It differs from both the Delco and the Bosch in that the heated sensing element lies outside the main channel of airflow in a bypass. Getting the sensing element into a bypass tube instead of having it in the main channel of airflow keeps the sensing element from impeding the flow of air into the engine. Being out of the main channel of airflow also reduces the build-up on the sensing element wire, eliminating the need for a burn-off cycle.

On GM applications, the Hitachi style MAF mounts directly on the throttle body assembly, which eliminates the possibility of an air leak occurring between the MAF and the throttle.

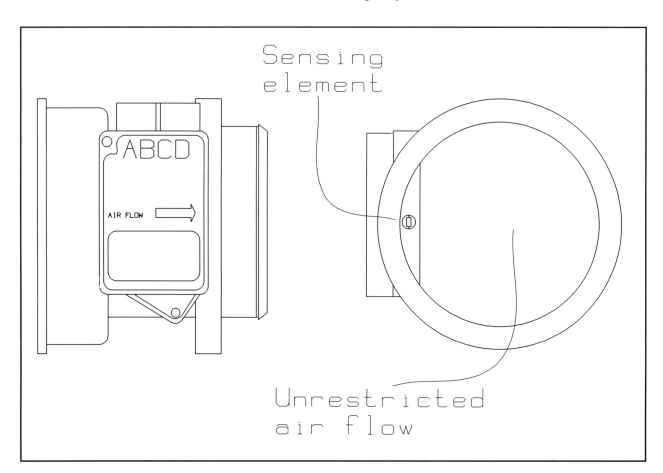

The Hitachi Mass Air Flow sensor is used by several Japanese manufacturers, by Ford and by GM. It is a highly dependable unit but its biggest advantage over all other air flow measuring devices is that there is no restriction to air flow created by the sensing element.

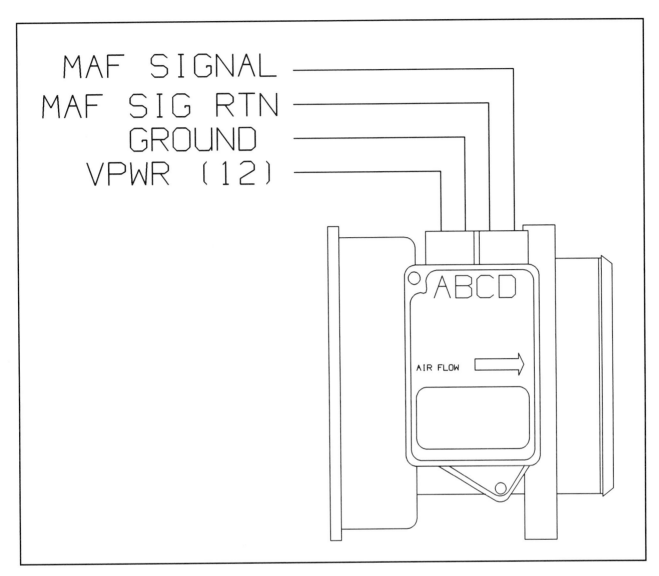

MAF SIGNAL
MAF SIG RTN
GROUND
VPWR (12)

ABCD

AIR FLOW

The latest incarnation of the mass air flow sensor are those based on a Hitachi design. These AMF place the sensor element in a bypass tube parallel to the main channel of air flow. The result is that the sensor has no impact on the air flow.

**Aftermarket**

There are a few aftermarket mass airflow sensors on the market, most designed to be used with retrofit systems. Tuned Port Injection Specialists offers a modified Bosch unit for GM 5.0 and 5.7 liter Tuned Port applications. Since this is basically a stock unit that has been modified for better airflow it should meet emission requirements in any state.

Professional Flow Technologies offers a replacement for the MAF used on the 1990-92 3.8 liter Ford Thunderbirds and the and the 1988-92 5.0 liter Mustangs. This series of parts is called the "Pro M Mass Air Flow Sensor." These MAF sensors are approved by the state of California (Res. Number D-242-1 dated 6/29/92).

**Electronic Components of Throttle Body Injection**

TBI systems also incorporate an assortment of other sensors.

**Throttle Position Sensor (TPS)**

The modern throttle position sensor is a potentiometer. There are three wires connected to the TPS—a 5 volt reference, a ground (sometimes called signal return), and the signal wire. As the throttle is opened the signal voltage will proportionately increase from a low of about .5 to a high of more than 4 volts.

The primary job of the TPS is to replace the accelerator pump.

Its settings and adjustments are probably best left alone when the intake manifold is replaced.

## Coolant Temperature Sensor

The coolant temperature sensor is a resistor known as a Negative Temperature Coefficient Thermistor. This type of resister responds dramatically to changes in temperature. On all domestic non-Ford applications, the resistance is about 100,700 ohms at -40 degrees C. The Ford negative temperature coefficient thermistor has a resistance at -40 degrees of 248,000 ohms. As the temperature increases the resistance decreases; as the resistance decreases the voltage of the coolant temperature circuit as measured by the computer decreases.

The coolant sensor circuit behaves a little differently from the electrical circuits with which most automotive technicians are familiar. A power supply (usually 5 volts) supplies a reference voltage to the circuit. Before leaving the computer, the five volt current passes through a fixed value resistor causing a voltage drop. The current then continues through the thermistor and on to ground where the voltage is zero. As the resistance of the thermistor changes the voltage on the wire between the fixed value resistor and the thermistor will also vary. The computer measures this voltage on the outbound side of the fixed value resistor to determine the temperature. When the computer sees a comparatively high voltage on the wire to the NTC thermistor it knows that the resistance in the thermistor is high; therefore, the temperature of the thermistor is low. A low voltage on this wire means that the resistance is low and therefore the temperature must be high.

Most applications use a coolant sensor at 100 degrees C and will have a resistance of about 200 ohms. Ford coolant temperature sensors will have a resistance of close to 1800 ohms at 100 degrees C. When the engine is cold, the wire carrying the five volt ref-

The Hitachi style MAF is used by several manufacturers including Ford and General Motors. Sleek and solidly built this sensor has nothing suspended across the main channel of air flow.

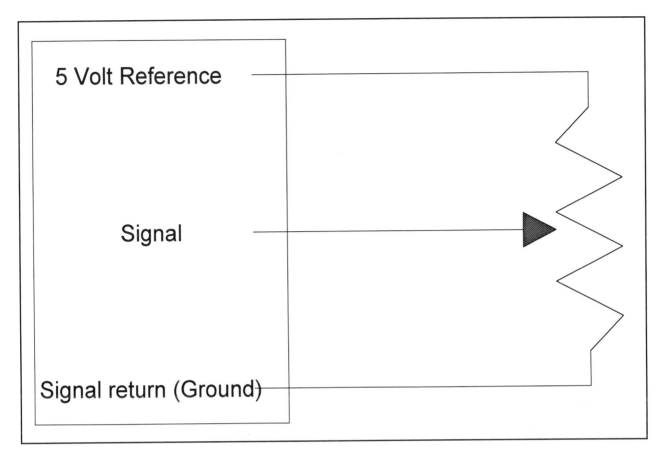

5 Volt Reference

Signal

Signal return (Ground)

The throttle position sensor tells the computer the throttle angle. This is translated by the computer into the estimated potential air flow which will then be compared to the RPM. The TPS is a potentiometer. There is a 5 volt reference wire, a ground wire and a third wire that sends a varying voltage to the computer. Any modification to the intake system must ensure the proper operation of the TPS.

erence will have about three to four volts on it, depending on the exact temperature of the engine coolant. As the engine warms up this voltage will drop, pulled low by the decreasing resistance in the coolant sensor.

The coolant temperature sensor replaces the choke of a carbureted car. When the computer detects a high voltage on the CTS wire it increases the pulse width to the injectors which enriches the mixture. In addition to enriching the air/fuel ratio it also causes the computer to permit additional timing advance when the indicated temperature is low.

**Track Trick**

Installing a 640ohm resistor across the terminals of the coolant sensor wiring harness with it disconnected from the coolant sensor will trick the computer into believing that the engine is not quite warmed up yet—about 145degrees F. The computer will respond by enriching the mixture and allowing more timing advance sooner. The net result is an increase in track performance for less than 50 cents.

A word of caution about this trick. Since on some applications the radiator cooling fan is controlled by the computer perception of coolant temperature, this trick should only be used for short runs at the drag strip. Prolonged use may cause severe overheating and engine damage since the computer would never turn on the radiator fan.

**Air Charge Temperature Sensor**

The air charge temperature sensor used on some throttle body applications measures the temperature, and therefore the density, of the air in the intake manifold. It measures the decrease in air charge density as the air moves through the warm intake manifold. This loss of density will result in less fuel being required for each cylinder

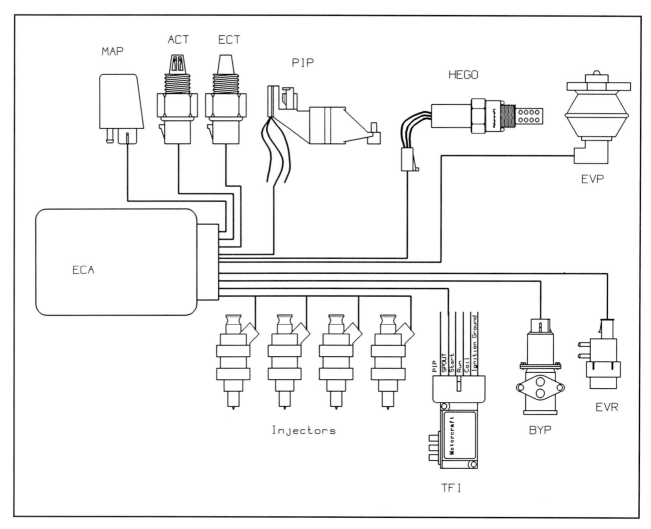

The position of electronic sensors after replacing or modifying the intake system is critical. Make sure they still perform their assigned task when your modifications are complete.

because the expansion will cause each cylinder to be charged with less oxygen.

The air charge temperature sensor is a negative temperature coefficient thermistor like the coolant temperature sensor. It is fed a five volt reference which is pulled low as the temperature drops and the as the resistance of the thermistor drops.

Many throttle body applications use an air temperature sensor which measures the temperature of the incoming air before it passes the throttle plates and enters the intake manifold. The term "air charge" is used to refer to the air inside the manifold, not in the air intake system upstream of the throttle plates.As a result calling it an "air charge temperature sensor" is inaccurate.

**Oxygen sensor**

The oxygen sensor measures the richness of the air/fuel mixture by measuring the oxygen content of the exhaust gases. A high oxygen level suggests that the engine is running lean while a low oxygen content suggests that the engine is running rich. A low oxygen content will cause the output voltage of the sensor to climb above 0.45 volts, a high oxygen content will cause the output voltage to drop below 0.45 volts. The computer uses this information to adjust the injector on-time for the best air/fuel ratio. The oxygen sensor and its operation are described more thoroughly in Chapter 14.

**Tach Signal**

The tach signal is used by the computer to synchronize and sometimes to sequence the injectors. This signal always originates with some component in the primary ignition system such as the ignition module or pick-up. In ad-

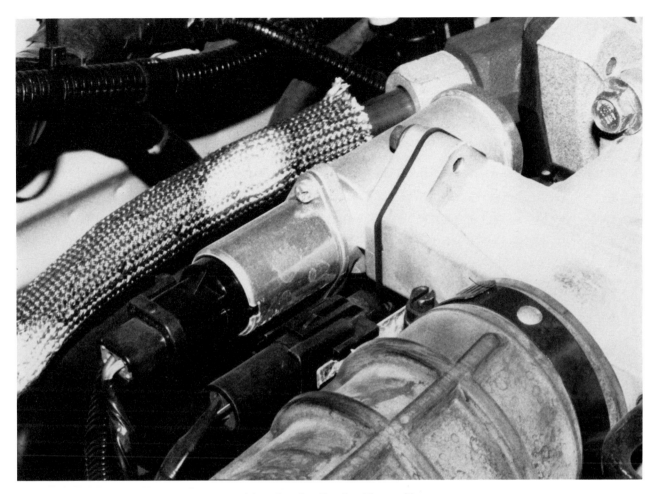

The throttle position sensor is located on the throttle shaft. This device replaces the function of the accellerator pump. This picture shows a typical location for the throttle position sensor, hidden. It is at the end of the connector closest to and above the large rubber tube.

dition to synchronizing the injectors the computer is designed to enter an enrichment mode at very high engine rpm.

## Thermistors

Thermistors are used to measure coolant temperature, air temperature, intake manifold temperature, car interior temperature and sun intensity. With all these different uses many share the same resistance specs.

### Almost all GM, AMC and Chrysler Thermistors

| | |
|---|---|
| -40 degrees F | = 100,700Ω |
| 0 degrees F | = 25,000Ω |
| 20 degrees F | = 13,500Ω |
| 40 degrees F | = 7,000Ω |
| 70 degrees F | = 3,400Ω |
| 100 degrees F | = 1,600Ω |
| 160 degrees F | = 450Ω |
| 212 degrees F | = 185Ω |

### Most Bosch Thermistors

| | |
|---|---|
| 14 degrees F | = 7,000-12,000Ω |
| 68 degrees F | = 2,000-3,000Ω |
| 122 degrees F | = 700-1,000Ω |
| 176 degrees F | = 250-400Ω |

### Most Ford Thermistors

| | |
|---|---|
| -40 degrees F | = 248,000Ω |
| 50 degrees F | = 58,750Ω |
| 100 degrees F | = 16,000Ω |
| 180 degrees F | = 2,850Ω |
| 212 degrees F | = 2,070Ω |

*NOTE:* These are examples and although they would work for most of the applications described, be sure to check the reference manual for the vehicle being tested.

## Considerations for manifold replacement
### Vacuum switches

Probably one of the most frustrating things in the world, other than sighting hundreds of deer during dove season, is trying to deal with the countless vacuum switches, reservoirs and delays installed on vehicles manufactured between 1970 and the present. The champion of this frustration has to be my wife's Cadillac. As much as we would like to escort these items to the nearest trash can, this is not recommended if the vehicle is ever going to see the street again. After years of beating around the bush and laxity of enforcement, the environmental powers that be are starting to seriously enforce rules concerning tampering.

Not too long ago I was in a performance parts store in my home town. I overheard a customer saying that although it was illegal for a professional to make modifications to the engine that would disable the emission control system, the consumer could still do it. Well guess what, in many jurisdictions today there is an underhood inspection that requires the inspector to fail a vehicle which

has been tampered with, and possibly levy fines, regardless of who made the modifications.

The vacuum switches referred to in the heading are used to control the application of vacuum, based on temperature. Often referred to as thermal vacuum switches, these were the bane of technicians for decades. Under the hood of every "emissions" equipped car there should be a vacuum rout-

If the intake manifold was originally set up for a carburetor there may be no provision for a coolant temperature sensor. Leaving the Coolant sensor out of the water jacket of the manifold would cause the computer to believe that the engine is much colder than it really is. The result would be similar to a carburetor running with the choke still on. If necessary the replacement, performance manifold can be modified by a ma-

chinist. The coolant temperature sensor should be located as close to the thermostat housing of the manifold as possible. This picture shows its stock location. (Keep in mind that in your jurisdiction just having everything in place may not be adequate, it may also be necessary to gain a California Air Resources Board Executive order number, a costly and time consuming task.)

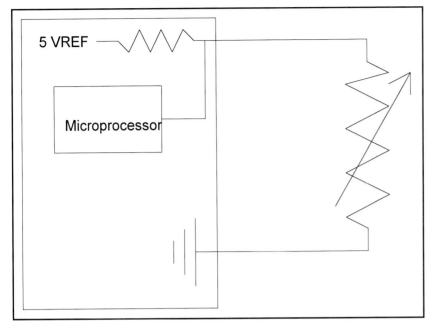

The coolant temperature sensor is usually located near the thermostat housing. If the thermostat is located in the intake manifold then it would be advisable to ensure that the replacement manifold will permit the coolant sensor to be located in the same position as the original manifold.

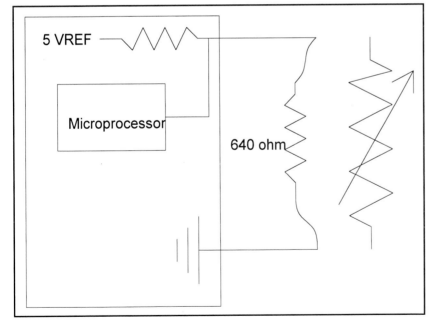

Now if you are interested in performance, and if you are reading this book you probably are, there is a little trick that can be done with the coolant temperature sensor circcuit. As the engine warms the resistance of the coolant temperature sensor is supposed to drop. As the resistance drops the computer leans out the mixture and retards the timing when the engine is under a load. For many performance applications stopping the drop of resistance at 640 ohms (or there about) can leave the engine with a little extra power on the track. NOTE CAUTION IN TEXT!

ing label. This vacuum routing diagram, I firmly believe, is viewed by painters as the "TEST YOUR PAINT GUN HERE" label. If your vacuum diagram has been painted over there are a couple of sources where you can get vacuum diagrams. One, of course is from the vehicle manufacturer, another is from Mitch-ell's Books. Remember that when dealing with emission testers, referees, and the other powers that be, the more the engine looks like it did the day it came off the assembly line, the less likely they are to look closely. I realize that this last statement could be interpreted as advocating illegal tampering. Actually, my concern is to convince these people that the legal modifications that are made are truly legal.

Make sure that if the vehicle is still used on the street the replacement manifold will accommodate the original thermal vacuum switches.

**Air temperature sensors**

If your vehicle is fuel injected there may be an air temperature sensor located on the intake manifold. Be sure to look at the existing manifold and make sure the new manifold has a place for this sensor. Failure to mount the air temperature sensor properly in the manifold, if required, can cause driveability problems.

**Air flow sensors**

Air flow sensors are used on some fuel injection systems that use one injector per cylinder. It is unlikely that you will ever have to give a great deal of thought to the mounting of this sensor. First, if you have a car with multipoint fuel injection you probably already have one of the best street performance manifolds available, and it has the factory mark on it. Secondly, if you are planning on replacing the manifold, the manufacturer of that new manifold has already made arrangements for the mounting of the airflow sensor. A word of caution: the distance between the air-

If your new intake manifold meets California Air Resources Board requirements all you will need to do is install all the components from the original manifold into the places provided in the new manifold. If you are not required to meet California Air Resources Board requirements for the vehicle you are modifying, the replacement manifold may not have a place to install the intake air temperature sensor. Leaving this sensor out, or simply allowing it to hang under the hood can create driveability or fuel economy problems. Note the location of the air temperature sensor on the original manifold and talk to a good machinist about creating a place for it in the new manifold.

flow sensor and the throttle plate is very critical. Keep the distance the same if possible. If the distance must be changed, move the sensor closer in the air stream to the throttle plates; increasing the distance may result in a lag, sag, or stumble on acceleration.

## Air pressure sensors
### Barometric sensor

There are two air pressure sensors that may be used in fuel injected engines. The first is the barometric pressure sensor or "baro" sensor. This sensor needs no attention when you replace the intake manifold, unless it happens to be mounted on the manifold. If it is mounted on the manifold, it just needs to find a home where its wires can still be connected.

### MAP sensors

The manifold absolute pressure (MAP) sensor needs to remain connected to the central plenum area of the intake manifold. Mounting of this device after the manifold transplant can be critical on a fuel injected car. Many fuel injected applications use this sensor for detecting engine load and airflow. If its connecting hose is longer than the stock configuration, a stumble or hesitation may result.

When modifications are done to increase airflow into the engine, the manifold pressure will rise as a result. The higher the manifold pressure, the more of a load the

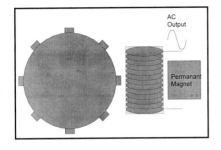

Left: Essential to the operation of the fuel injection system is the crankshaft speed sensor. This is located either in the distributor or on the crankshaft.

MAP will tell the computer the engine is under. At first this may appear to be a problem. However, at least for a reasonably sensible street modification, there has been an increase in air volume entering the engine (especially off-idle) and the engine has a need for extra fuel. The MAP tells the computer that the engine is under an additional load and the computer puts extra fuel into the engine. In most cases the amount of extra fuel is the amount required by the engine.

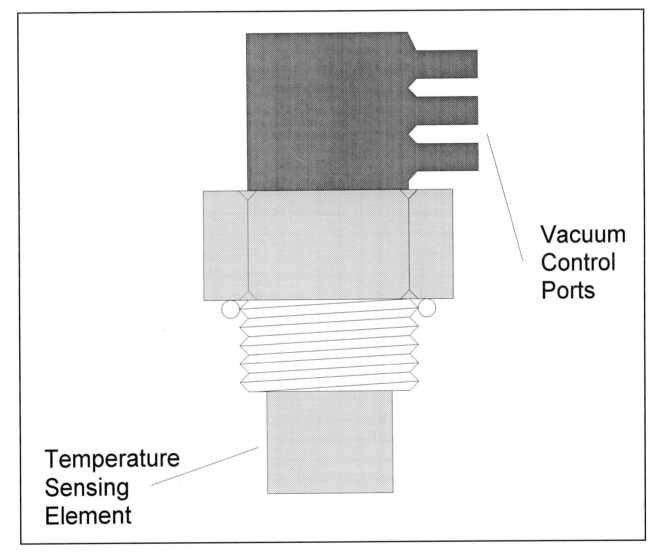

Vacuum Control Ports

Temperature Sensing Element

Thermal vacuum control switches have been the curse of the automotive technician since the early 1970's. These devices have controlled everything from ignition timing to intake manifold heat. If the engine you are modifying is destined exclusively for the track then the extent of the modifications are such that you probably will eliminate all the devices controlled by these switches. If the car is going to be used on the street with a state provided decoration on the front bumper, then these devices must be left in place and properly connected. If the replacement manifold does not provide for installation of the thermal vacuum switches visit your local machinist and have him provide places for their installation. This may be expensive but it is cheaper than the hassles of dealing with the local emission control agency. (Note: if the manifold has not been formally approved by the California Air Resources Board then no amount of modification will make it legal in many jurisdictions. Check with your local emission control agency before making any expensive purchases.)

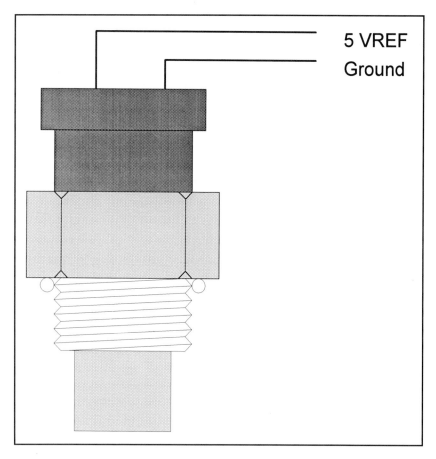

5 VREF

Ground

Another device found in the intake manifold of many fuel injection systems is the manifold air temperature sensor. The information from the MAT sensor is critical to the computer selecting the correct injector on time as the density of the air changes due to temperature.

The accuracy of the MAP sensor is crucial to the proper performance of the throttle body injection system. When stock intake manifolds are replaced with the performance variety the intake manifold pressure (vacuum) curve will change. In some cases, however, replacement of the intake manifold can cause the MAP sensor to demand improper fuel delivery at certain rpm's. Since most replacement manifolds are bought off the shelf rather than being custom designed, you may be able to get recommendations on how to compensate for this problem from the intake manifold manufacturer. If not, here are some tips.

Changes in pressure: Generally replacement manifolds will cause an increase in manifold pressure. This will cause the MAP sensor to inform the fuel injection computer that the engine is under a greater load than it really is. As a result the fuel system will tend to put in more fuel than is normally required for a given engine speed and load condition. If we lived on the aforementioned perfect world all performance manifolds would yield manifold pressure changes that were exactly proportionate to the change in fuel demand required for the change in airflow. All things would remain in balance. However, in our world, there will be a point in the rpm and power curves where the engine will be lean. This can hurt performance and even damage the engine.

Left: Any modifications to the engine's intake system must provide for retention of the air measuring sensors. This Ford engine uses a mass air flow sensor located near the air cleaner. If there are any modifications made to the intake system there should be no air allowed to enter between the MAF and the throttle assembly. Any air that does will not be measured by the computer and will cause the engine to run lean.

Multipoint and most throttle body fuel injected engines do not control the idle speed of the engine by changing the throttle position. Instead idle speed is controlled by the amount of air allowed to bypass the throttle through an air bypass control. Ford uses a computer controlled solenoid to control idle speed. If the stock manifold is modified nothing should be done to this bypass air control.

There are two categories of MAP sensors. While they operate differently with respect to electronics, how the computer assesses the information from those sensors is the same.

This is the location of the MAP sensor on an Oldsmobile Quad 4 engine. Note that there is a very short vacuum hose running from the intake plenum to the MAP sensor. Lengthening this hose may cause a hesitation or stumble.

There are three ways to reduce or eliminate this problem. First, those who have lots of time, fuel, a test track, and little if anything of real value to do, they can experiment with changes in fuel pressure. While altering the fuel pressure may cause the engine to run rich at some points in the rpm curve, affect emissions, and even be illegal for a street car, depending on jurisdiction, it can resolve performance problems. Depending on the application, fuel pressure can be altered by replacing the stock fuel pressure regulator with an adjustable aftermarket one or, in the case of GM TBI applications, by disassembling the regulator and shimming the spring.

The second way is through a programmable read only memory (PROM) replacement. There are several manufacturers of replacement PROM's for GM and Ford computers. These modify the enrichment points and timing map to take advantage of performance modifications. Call Hypertech or one of their competitors and see what they recommend.

The third way is by replacing the stock computer with an adjustable computer. This would allow you to "dial in" the correct enrichment curve and timing curve. Be aware that replacing the PROM or the computer may be illegal for street cars in your jurisdiction.

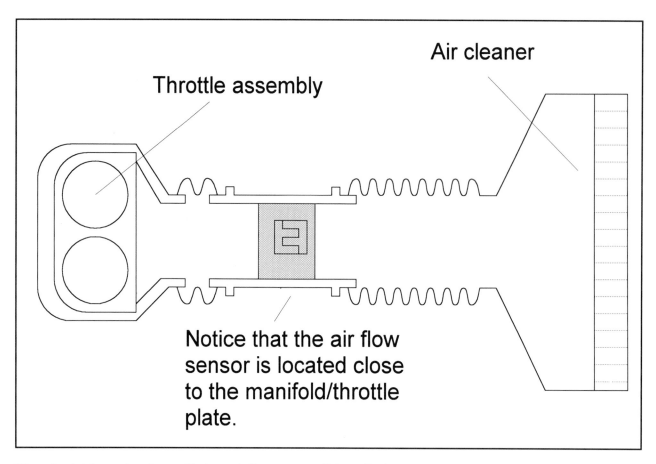

Throttle assembly

Air cleaner

Notice that the air flow sensor is located close to the manifold/throttle plate.

When the intake system is modified the location or relocation of the mass air flow sensor will be critical to engine performance.

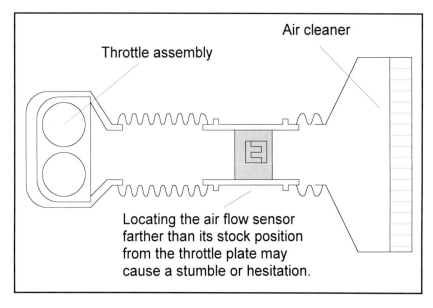

Throttle assembly

Air cleaner

Locating the air flow sensor farther than its stock position from the throttle plate may cause a stumble or hesitation.

Moving the MAF to a location different from that determined by the manufacturer may have negative results in performance.

# Chapter 5
## Throttle Body Fuel Injection

### Just the basics of TBI

The modern "electronic" fuel injector is a normally closed solenoid operated valve. On most domestic applications the injector is connected to a 12 volt power source and the computer connects it to ground in order to energize and open the injector. There are two major categories of injectors used by domestic applications. The first is the "top feed" or high pressure injector. This injector is used on some early Ford V-6 and V-8 applications as well as the 1984 through 1986 four cylinder Chrysler applications.

The other type of injector is known as a side or bottom feed injector. These are used exclusively on the TBI applications at a typical fuel pressure of between 10 and 20 PSI. Only one of these injectors is used to fuel an entire four cylinder engine and two are used on the low pressure TBI equipped V-6's and V-8's.

The computer controls the energizing of the injectors with transistors located in the com-

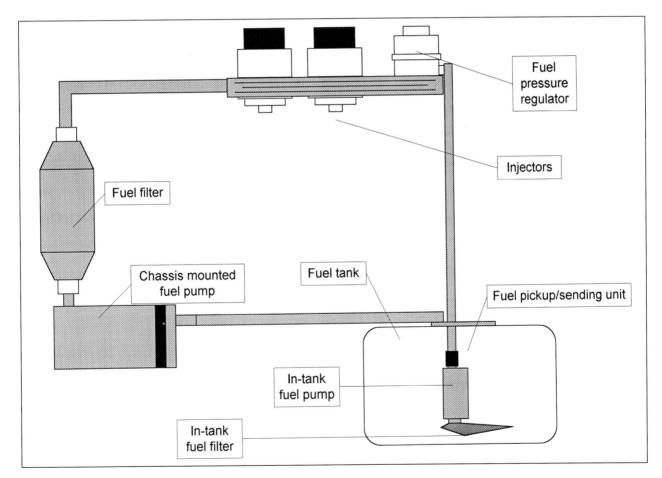

Throttle body injection was introduced in the early 1980's. At first this appeared to be a stop-gap measure to allow time for the development of multipoint fuel injection systems to rival those of Bosch. By the middle 1980's aftermarket, performance applications became available. A throttle body injection system usually has good low end performance like a carburetor with the added advantage of not having a venturi to impede air flow at high engine speeds.

puter. On TBI (a term used by GM, Chrysler and most import applications) and CFI (a Ford term) applications, an injector opens every time there is a primary ignition pulse. This means that on a one injector TBI the injector opens every time a spark plug fires. This also means that there is an air pulse to drag the injected fuel into the combustion chamber every time the injector opens. On the two injector applications the injectors will alternate so that each injector opens every other time a spark plug fires.

## Fuel Lines

All of these components are connected by hoses or steel lines. The hose that runs from the fuel pump to the fuel rail is called the supply line. Somewhere in the supply line is the fuel filter. The line that runs from the fuel pressure regulator back to the fuel tank is called the return line. Although in most cases these lines or hoses are ignored during a troubleshooting procedure, it should be kept in mind that they can develop problems such as restrictions, kinks and collapsing. Because of the higher pressures and volumes associated with fuel injection systems when compared to carburetors, do not use standard fuel line when replacing hoses on a fuel injected car. Always use a high pressure rated fuel injection line.

## Electronic Control Module

The computer is the brain of the fuel injection system and is divided into three major sections.

The ROM Section—The ROM section of the computer contains the principle set of instructions for the on-board computer to follow. This is the section that says, "When I see this happen, I have to make that happen." The microprocessor that contains these ROM instructions is a non-volatile chip. This means that the programming designed

The top feed injector first entered mass production with the Bosch D-Jetronic fuel injection system of the late 1960's. In these injectors the fuel enters at the top of the injector, passes through the injector and sprays out of the tip. The typical fuel pressure in systems where these injectors are used is about 35 to 45psi. These are still commonly used in multipoint fuel injected engines, but have been seldom used since 1985 in throttle body injected engines.

This is a "side feed" or bottom feed injector. The fuel enters the through the screens on the side of the injector turns a corner and sprays through the tip. Since the throttle body injector, both the top feed and the side feed, sits above the main channel of air flow they do not increase air flow restriction as does the carburetor venturi.

into it cannot be erased by disconnecting the power.

The PROM is the "calibration" chip in the computer. The PROM works along with the ROM to fine tune the functions of fuel and timing control for the specific application. The PROM is also a non-volatile memory. The Prom contains information about size of the engine, type of transmission, size and weight of the car, rolling resistance, drag coefficient and final drive ratio. Several aftermarket manufacturers such as Hypertech produce chips which offer improved performance. Laws concerning the use of these chips differ from one state to another, in general they are legal only for off-road use. The effect of these chips on the fuel injection and timing control system is similar to the effect of re-curving the distributor and re-jetting the carburetor in the old days.

RAM or Random Access Memory has three primary functions in the computer. The first function is to act as the computer's "scratch pad." Whenever a mathematical calculation needs to be done the computer uses the RAM. The second function is to store information about the trend or oxygen sensor reading caused by vacuum leaks, fuel-diluted oil, and similar air/fuel ratio problems while the engine is shut down or operating in open loop. The third function is to store diagnostic codes when a system fault has been detected. The RAM chips are volatile memories.

## Modes Of Operation

General Motors fuel injection has eight distinct modes of operation. Ford and Chrysler have similar modes but may use different names.

1. Shut Down
2. Start-up
3. Open Loop
4. Closed Loop
5. Enrichment

The basic functions of the carburetor are replaced by sensors and injectors on fuel injected engines. Unlike a carburetor the fuel injection system cannot meter the correct amount of fuel on its own. Information about engine speed, temperature, load and driver demand must be sent to a central processing unit, or computer.

6. Enleanment
7. Fuel Cutoff
8. Clear flood

## Shut Down

The computer enters the Shut Down Mode when the ignition switch is shut off for more than two seconds. For the first two seconds after the engine is shut off the computer remains powered up and the fuel pump remains activated. After the two seconds pass, all power is removed from the computer circuits, with two exceptions. The first exception is the diagnostic RAM, the other is the information about oxygen sensor trends.

## Start-Up

The "Start-up" mode is entered while the engine is being cranked. Timing becomes locked in at an initial value, and the air/fuel ratio is enriched slightly to expedite starting. This mode of operation continues for a second or two after starting to ensure that the engine will continue to run.

## Open Loop

After the engine is started, it will operate in the open loop mode for several seconds to several minutes, depending on the temperature of the engine and oxygen sensor. In open loop all engine sensors except the oxygen sensor are actively providing information about running requirements.

The computer is watching the coolant sensor, the oxygen sensor, and its internal timer, to determine when the engine will be ready to operate in closed loop. Three things must occur before the computer will enter closed loop. The coolant temperature sensor must reach a temperature specified for closed loop operation by the PROM; a certain programmed time from start up must pass; and the computer must know that the oxygen sensor is warmed up, which it does

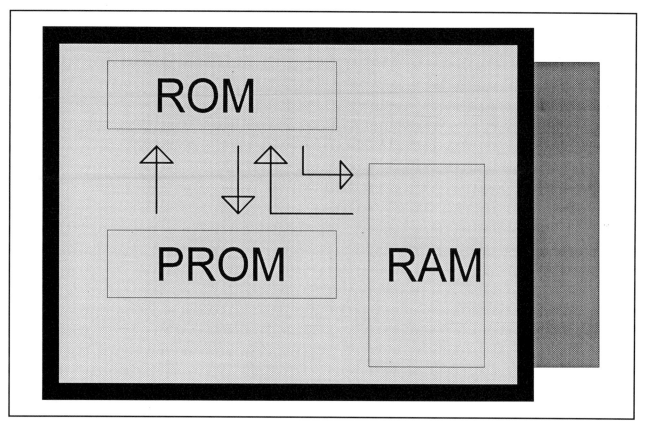

The carburetor is capable of measuring air flow and metering the proper amount of fuel into the intake system. The fuel injection system cannot do this. The input sensors are monitored by the computer which selects an injector on-time. In a very real way the sensors and computer of a modern fuel injection system are just like a carburetor. The nice thing about these sytems is that they are able to adapt to some rather radical street perfomance intake and exhaust options with little or no modification to the fuel injection system.

by monitoring its output voltage. When the voltage increases above 450 millivolts, drops below, then increases again, it is assumed that the oxygen sensor is warmed up.

During open loop operation, the coolant temperature sensor is telling the computer about leaner and leaner requirements in the air/fuel ratio as the engine warms up, performing much the same function that a choke performs on a carbureted engine. The MAP is telling the computer the quantity of air that is entering the engine and about any changes in engine load. The air temperature sensor is updating the computer on changes in fuel requirements based on the density of the air. The throttle position sensor is keeping the computer abreast of what power changes the driver expects. As the TPS voltage increases, the computer will assume it is because the throttle is opening and the computer will respond by increasing the amount of fuel that is entering the engine.

To summarize open loop operation:

• Coolant sensor monitored for: engine temperature for entering closed loop; "choke" air/fuel ratio.

• MAF/MAP monitored for: flow of air into the engine; engine load.

• Air charge temperature monitored for changes in the density of the air.

• Throttle position sensor monitored for changes in driver demand and engine load based on driver demand.

**Closed Loop**

The only real difference between open loop and closed loop operation is that during closed loop the oxygen sensor is being used by the computer to monitor exhaust oxygen content so that the air/fuel ratio can be constantly trimmed to 14.7:1. Under normal driving conditions the computer is in the Closed Loop mode the majority of the time.

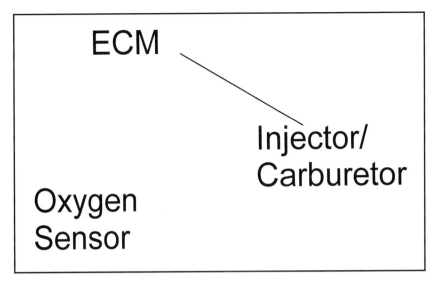

Modern fuel injection and factory carburetor systems are designed to closely follow guidelines for emissions. These fuel injection systems use the oxygen sensor to monitor the air/fuel ratio. Several conditions are necessary for the this monitoring to occur. First, the coolant temperature sensor must indicate that the engine is at or near operating temperature. Secondly, a specified amount of time must have passed and finally the oxygen sensor must be warm. Before these conditions are met the engine will be operating in an open loop mode. In open loop the oxygen sensor is ignored.

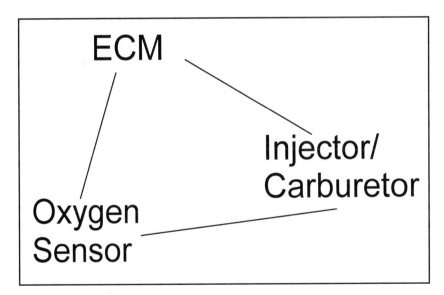

When the engine temperature approaches operating temperature the fuel injection or electronic carburetor computer will begin to take information from the oxygen sensor. When this occurs the engine, computer and oxygen sensor is said to be operating in closed loop.

## Enrichment

The fifth mode of operation is called the enrichment mode. The computer can enter the enrichment mode from either open or closed loop. When entering this mode from closed loop the computer will ignore the oxygen sensor until the engine operating conditions once again permit closed loop operation. Enrichment mode is entered when any one of the following conditions are met:

a. Wide Open Throttle: when throttle position sensor voltage goes over about 80 percent or 4 volts the air fuel ratio is enriched to provide extra power.

b. High Engine Load: when the MAP sensor voltage approaches four volts (Ford approaching 150 Hertz), the computer will enter the enrichment mode, assuming that the engine is under a heavy load.

c. When the coolant temperature sensor detects an overheating engine, the enrichment mode is entered to cool the combustion chamber and thereby assist in cooling the operating temperature of the engine.

## Enleanment

When the TPS indicates a nearly closed throttle, and when the MAP indicates that there is very little or no load on the engine, the computer will lean out the air fuel ratio to something leaner than 14.7:1. This serves two purposes. First, this is one means of conserving fuel to increase economy of operation. Second, the conditions which cause the computer to enter the enleanment mode are also the engine operating conditions which cause high levels of CO and HC emissions. Leaning out the air/fuel ratio reduces the level of these emissions.

## Fuel Cut-Off

When the throttle is closed and the MAP indicates a negative load is on the engine, as in heavy deceleration, the computer will cut off the injector(s). Again CO and HC emissions are reduced as the engine rpm's are decreasing. The computer will remain in fuel cut-off during heavy deceleration until the engine drops below about 1500rpm.

### Clear Flood

Back in 1969 my dad taught me that when I thought my car was flooded I should hold the accelerator pedal to the floor in order to maximize airflow and pray that the engine starts before the battery goes dead. Unfortunately the natural response for the computer is to notice the increase in TPS voltage, assume that the driver wants to accelerate, and dump still more fuel through the injectors flooding the engine even more. To prevent this the computer has a "Clear Flood" program. When the engine is being cranked and the throttle is more than 80 percent toward wide open, the clear flood mode is entered which either turns off the injector(s) completely or leans the air/fuel ratio to approximately 20:1.

### Summary of Modes

Although each of these modes of operation is a separate program within the computer, they all act together to ensure good driveability, low emissions and good fuel economy.

# Chapter 6
# Multipoint Point Fuel Injection (MPFI)

The use of multipoint fuel injection on late model vehicles is the most exciting thing to happen to automotive breathing systems since the advent of the downdraft carburetor. Essentially a multipoint fuel injection system does not do anything that a throttle body injection system does not do, it just does it more accurately.

## The fuel supply system

The fuel supply system begins with a fuel tank. Many of these fuel tanks have a lining that can be damaged by fuel additives containing methanol or methyl hydrate. Most late model electronic fuel injection (EFI) systems place the fuel pump in the fuel tank. This might be only a supply pump to a chassis mounted pump, or it

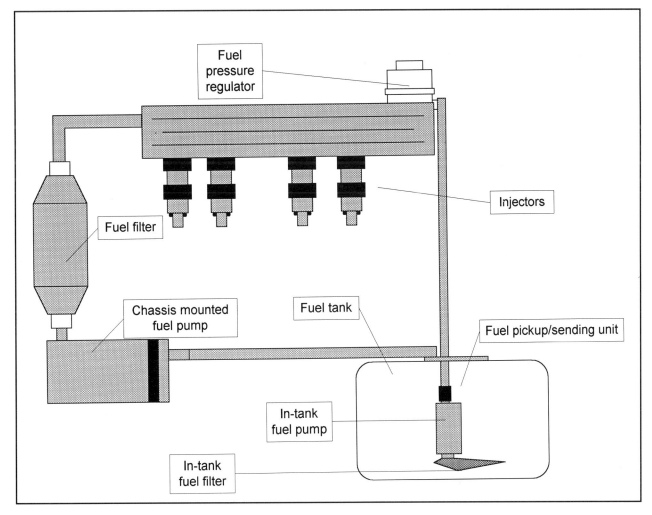

Multipoint fuel injection systems offers a lot of flexibility in intake manifold design. From the perspective of intake manifold design the biggest advantage of multipoint fuel injection is that there is no need to keep the fuel suspended in the air traveling toward the combustion chamber. This means that the intake can be designed with only the maximizing of air flow in mind.

might be the main supply pump for the entire system.

The fuel pumps are typically able to flow about one-half gallon (gal) per minute. A stock 350 Chevrolet engine will flow about 405 cubic feet or 3029gal of air per minute at 5000rpm. The perfect air/fuel ratio is about 10,000-gal of air to 1gal of fuel. Based on this ratio, 3,029gal of fuel will require only 0.3gal of fuel each minute. The fuel pumps, therefore, are capable of flowing 1.7 times as much fuel as the engine will ever demand.

If there are major intake manifold, exhaust, cam, and piston modifications to the engine, you may need to consider replacing the fuel pump(s) with higher volume units. To determine the required fuel pump volume you must first know the maximum airflow for the engine. Use the following formula which will somewhat over-estimate the airflow:

**Air flow=**
**[ (cubic inch displacement x**
**maximum RPM) / 3456] x 1.2**

A modified 350ci Chevrolet engine would therefore have a maximum non-supercharged airflow of 608cfm. Multiply this by 7.5 to find how many gallons of air will flow per minute. This means that our Chevy 350 would draw 4,560gal of air per minute. Divide this by 10,000 to determine the required fuel flow rate. Our example engine would require a fuel flow rate of 0.4560gal. At first glance it appears that a flow rate of 0.5gal would be adequate. However, when the engine is under a load the fuel pressure increases and the injector on-time increases. In a performance application the pumps should be capable of keeping up with demand at a 5,000:1 air fuel ratio. The fuel flow rate for a 350 performance engine should be between 0.912 and 1gal per minute.

Many modern engines use multipoint electronic fuel injection. The injectors are located in the intake manifold very close to the cylinder head. This is an almost ideal position for mixing the air and the fuel. Intake manifold designs become limited only by the imagination of the designer.

After the fuel pumps there is a fuel filter. The easiest way to determine if the flow rate capacity of the fuel filter is adequate is with a fuel pressure gauge mounted on the injection system fuel supply line near the fuel rail. If the pressure drops at times of maximum fuel demand, then the filter or the lines have an inadequate flow rate. This, of course, assumes that the flow rate of the fuel pump is adequate.

From the fuel filter the fuel is carried to the fuel rail. Some Ford applications use a small plastic and steel tube as a fuel rail. This arrangement may yield an inadequate fuel flow if the engine has been highly modified. For most applications the fuel flow through the fuel rail should be wholly adequate.

Next come the injectors. For the most part, the injector flow rate will be adequate even when the intake manifold has been replaced. Different electronic fuel injection applications use different injectors having different flow rates. The Chevy 350 uses an injector with a flow rate of about 22 lbs/hour. The '89 Thunderbird Supercharged 3.8 Super Coupe uses an injector which flows 32 lbs/hour. At first glance this might seem to be a favorable improvement, yet the end result of putting the T-Bird injectors in the Corvette might well turn out to be the same as raising the float level too high on a carburetor. Injectors cost $50+ on the cheap! For a V-8 this means a minimum of $400 to replace the injectors, and a more realistic figure would be closer to $600. This investment would show almost no positive gain in performance and may cause driveability problems. Your money would be better spent on cam-shafts and "re-curving the distributor."

Required injector flow rates can be calculated using the following formula:

**lb/hour=**
**[ (max. horsepower x**
**brake specific fuel consumption) /**
**number of injectors]**

The brake specific fuel consumption is the amount of fuel in pounds that it takes to create 1hp for one hour. This figure is typically 0.45 on a normally aspirated engine and 0.55 on a turbocharged or supercharged one.

Using a horsepower figure of 220 for a 3.0 SHO the formula would look like this:

$$\frac{220 \times 0.45}{6} = \text{approximately 16.5 lb / hour}$$

A highly modified turbocharged engine with a maximum horsepower of 500 would look like this:

$$\frac{500 \times 0.55}{8} = \text{approximately 35 lb / hour}$$

An engine like this would require either an aftermarket fuel injection system or an alternative fuel source when operating under boost. To solve this problem, some performance modifiers have rigged the cold start injector to energize when the turbo goes into boost. The problem with this is that there is no way to control accurately the amount of additional fuel, and not all applications you might be turbocharging have a cold start injector. Micro-Dynamics builds an electronically controlled auxiliary fuel injector for situations like this.

**Fuel pressure regulator**

The fuel pressure regulator ensures the proper flow rate through the injector. A rise in fuel pressure will increase the flow rate, while a low fuel pressure will decrease it. On the stock "typical" MPFI system the fuel pressure is regulated at 35psi with no load on the engine. As the engine is put under a load the fuel pressure increases in one step, jumping up to between 40-

This is the fuel pressure regulator from a multipoint injected Ford. The tube rising vertically from the center of the regulator is the "vacuum" port that goes to the manifold.

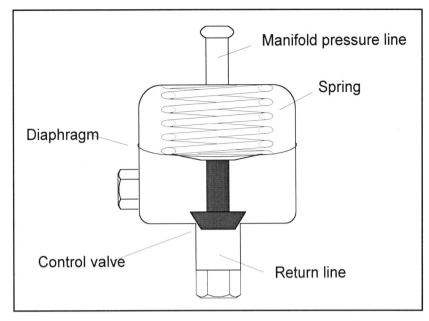

The fuel pressure regulator is reponsible for maintaining the proper pressure differential between the pressure of the gasoline and the pressure present in the intake manifold. The typical pressure differential is about 55-65psig (pounds per square inch gauge). At an idle the pressure in the intake manifold is only about 5psia (pounds per square inch absolute). Therefore the pressure differential is equal to the difference in psia between the air in the manifold and the psia of the fuel. If the gauge psi of the fuel is 40psi, then the absolute pressure of the fuel is 55psi. If the vacuum in the manifold at an idle is 20 in Hg then the pressure in the manifold is -10psi gauge. The pressure differential is therefore 50psi. As the throttle is opened the pressure in the intake manifold rises to nearly atmospheric. This means the pressure in the manifold has been increased by 10psi. To maintain the proper fuel flow rate the fuel pressure must also rise by 10psi. A "vacuum" line from the intake to the fuel pressure regulator must be present and not of excessive length to accomplish this.

This fuel pressure regulator was found in an ancient pyramid in the Yucatan. Actually it is from a Bosch D-Jetronic fuel injection system. The bolt on top and the lock nut below it were used to set fuel pressure. When the manifold is replaced and other modifications are made for performance-only use you may decide that it is better to set the fuel pressure for maximum speed and power. This may cause the engine to run rich at an idle or at low speeds, but perform well under full power/load conditions.

The vacuum line that runs from the manifold to the fuel pressure regulator is essential to maintain the proper pressure differential between the fuel and air in the intake manifold.

45psi. There are two types of fuel pressure regulators currently on the market which can significantly improve power.

The first is an adjustable fuel pressure regulator. Dyno tests show that horsepower and acceleration improve with about a 20-25 percent increase in fuel pressure.

While at the track with this unit installed, you will need to disconnect the oxygen sensor. When the computer enters the closed loop mode, the oxygen sensor would report the extra enrichment caused by the higher fuel pressure to the computer. The injector pulse width would then be shortened, leaning the air/fuel ratio, defeating the benefits of the higher fuel pressure. Disconnecting the oxygen sensor would either keep the computer from entering closed loop or deliver a "neutral" air/fuel ratio signal to the computer if it does.

MicroDynamics of England builds a "rising rate" fuel pressure regulator. This unit is adjustable and accurately tracks manifold pressure to alter fuel pressure to precisely meet engine demand. Again street legality is highly questionable so you might want to save it for the track. The advantage of the rising rate regulator is good top end performance without sacrificing a good idle. The U.S. price for the Microdynamics rising rate regulator is about $300.

Other companies which market 45psi or adjustable regulators include Digital Fuel Injection of Farmington Hills, Michigan, and Hypertech.

Changing fuel pressure is like changing a carburetor's float level. Raising the float level a little can increase an engines performance; raising it a lot can destroy it. You will need to play around with it a little to determine the fuel pressure that is right for your engine.

So called "Street/Strip" modifications always give the best performance improvements when

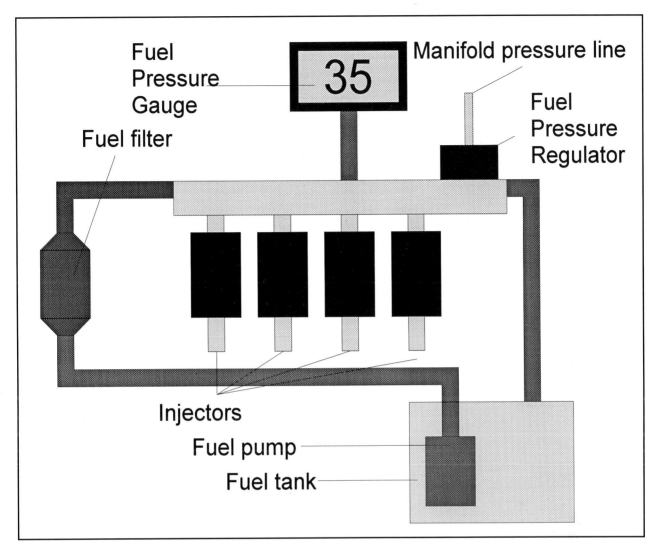

Fuel Pressure Gauge

35

Manifold pressure line

Fuel Pressure Regulator

Fuel filter

Injectors

Fuel pump

Fuel tank

The "rising rate" fuel pressure regulator uses increasing manifold pressure to increase the fuel pressure. Unlike most stock fuel pressure regulators which raise the fuel pressure in a single step the rising rate regulator increases the fuel pressure at the same rate that the manifold pressure increases. Thus, the pressure differential between the air in the manifold and the fuel is a constant.

two or more are planned and executed together. Keep in mind that the power from an internal combustion engine comes from its ability to gulp, ignite and expand air. Increasing the fuel pressure reaps maximum benefit when coupled with one of the engine breathing modifications mentioned earlier. Again, it is easy to put in more fuel, but the power comes from more air and more air is hard to put in.

### The computer

Today's automotive computers fall into two general categories: analog and digital. The use of analog computers dates back to the sixties. The analog computer is a single task device that is designed to convert variable voltage or variable frequency into a variable output. This variable output controls an output actuator such as a fuel injector. The processing from the input signal to the output signal is handled through variations in voltages and frequencies.

The digital computer has become the staple of automotive electronics. This is typically a multi-task device that takes variable voltage or frequency input signals, converts them into digitally coded information which the computer uses to decide how to control the output actuators.

There are five sections of a digital computer, as applied to fuel injection systems:

1. INPUT ANALOG TO DIGITAL (A-D) CONVERTERS
2. READ ONLY MEMORY (ROM) and PROGRAMMABLE READ ONLY MEMORY (PROM)
3. RANDOM ACCESS MEMORY (RAM)
4. CLOCK GENERATOR
5. OUTPUT DRIVERS

The digital computer gathers information from the sensors in analog form, as varying voltages or frequencies. These analog signals are then processed through the analog to a digital (A-D) converter which changes the variable voltage and frequency inputs into coded digital information. In binary code this information goes to the Central Processing Unit (CPU).

From these inputs the CPU determines the need for fuel, air injection, ignition timing and all of the other processes controlled by the computer, by comparing the input values to a set of reference values stored in the ROM. After making a basic determination of these needs the CPU then consults the PROM in order to fine tune these needs to the vehicle in which the computer is installed.

Should the ROM need to perform any mathematical computations, store information to compensate for engine or component wear, or store Fault Codes, it uses the RAM.

After the input information is processed, simple on-off signals are sent to the various actuators by the output section, to control their operations. The output section is a series of driver transistors which act as relays to switch on and off large currents through the actuators.

The clock generator provides a tempo at which functions can occur. It acts much like a symphony conductor pacing and synchronizing computer operations.

Because fuel injection systems do not use a venturi to

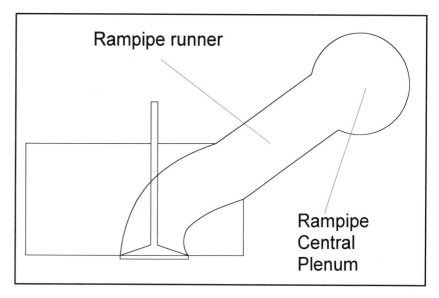

Rampipe runner

Rampipe Central Plenum

The "ram pipe" manifold is one of the more common designs used in multipoint fuel injection systems. In this design the air is gathered in a large central plenum and distributed through individual pipes to the intake valve. Most non-performance passenger cars use this design.

meter fuel flow and because the injectors are located just above the intake valve, the multipoint fuel injection system offers an opportunity for a great deal of creativity to the intake manifold designer.

One of the most unique designs is the manifold located on the Ford 3.0 SHO engine. This manifold uses long intake runners when the engine is operating at slow speeds and short intake runners when the engine is operating at high speeds. The computer switches from the long runners to the short ones at about 2200rpm, by grounding a solenoid that allows vacuum to flow to a servo that closes off one set of runners while opening the second set.

## Ram pipe

Ram pipe manifolds gather the air in a central plenum. As the throttle is opened the pressure in the manifold rises, making "high pressure" air available to the individual plenum runners. With these manifolds, air at equal pressure is available at all the intake runners, but the in-

take runners are not necessarily tuned precisely to the needs of the individual cylinders. There are many stock examples of this type of manifold, ranging from the relatively meek 3.0 liter GM engine to the relatively wild tuned port engines.

There are times that I like to quote higher authorities. These are times when I feel inadequate to properly expound on a point. The *Bosch Automotive Handbook* (2nd Edition) says this on the subject of ram pipe induction: "The energy balance is characterized by the fact that the intake work of the piston is converted into kinetic energy of the column of gas upstream of the intake valve, and this kinetic energy, in turn, is converted into fresh charge compression work." Okay, right, let us translate that into English. The low pressure area created by the dropping piston transfers energy from the movement of the piston to the air upstream of the intake valve. This energy becomes momentum of the moving air mass. If the amount of energy transferred from the moving piston is greater

The "Tuned Port" injection system of General Motors gets its name from the intake manifold design.

In the tuned port manifold the air is gathered in a central plenum then sent along runners to resonance chambers. These resonance chambers then feed the air to the cylinders. This design tunes the intake system to the wave length of the air flow pulses. Since the wave length of the air flow changes as the velocity and mass of air flow increases, what is an ideal length for one wave length is not an ideal length for another. The Ford SHO engine features a twin set of tuned runners. One set of runners is used at low engine speeds while the other set is used at higher engine speeds.

than the amount of energy required to fill the cylinder to atmospheric pressure, then "supercharging" of the cylinder will occur. All North American manufacturers use this type of manifold on their multipoint fuel injected engines.

For those of you that remember "My Mother the Car," these manifolds can be very frustrating. In the first place, since most of the engines in the modern "Q-ship" wannabe are small, their manifolds tend to be designed for maximum performance right from the factory. Secondly, you will have no luck finding replacement manifolds for most of the engines designed since the beginning of the eighties. There are plenty available for the designs of the fifties and sixties that are still in production—the 350's the 302's. There are none available for engines like the 3800GM, the 3.0 SHO Ford. In talking to representatives from intake manifold manufacturers, I have discovered that they believe that people would not do major performance modifications to these engines. Also, any modified manifold has to have approval from the California Air Resources Board (CARB), the California Bureau of Auto Repair (BAR) and the federal Environmental Protection Agency (EPA). The cost of all of these certifications can run into many, many thousands of dollars. Besides, how could they improve on many of these manifolds considering the legal limitations on engine modification?

## Tuned port

There has been much ado about the Tuned Port Fuel Injection system of General Motors. The fact is that there are many "tuned port" engines on the road. What distinguishes the tuned port manifold from the ram pipe manifold is the use of a resonance receiver. To again quote from the *Bosch Automotive Handbook*, "In tuned-intake tube charging, groups of cylinders with the same ignition intervals

The Ford SHO engine may mark the beginning of a new emphasis on performance. When the little old lady came from Pasadena performance meant putting large chunks of iron in large chunks of iron. To me and my contemporaries that meant power. Today power comes from maximizing the air flow in and out of smaller engines. The SHO engine is only 3.0 liters, less than half the size of many of the "powerhouses" of the 1960's.

are connected to resonance receivers via short tubes. These resonance receivers communicate with the atmosphere or a common receiver via tuned tubes, and act as Helm-holtz resonators." I am sure you would have said it just that way, but not I. Let me see if something a little more straight forward works better.

"Tuned" intake systems group cylinders that are equally spaced in the ignition cycle together. As a simple example of this imagine an inline four cylinder engine. Cylinders 1 and 4 are companion cylinders as are 2 and 3. Companion cylinders are cylinders in which the pistons are always at the same position in the cylinder. If piston number 1 is halfway through an upward stroke, compression, in the cylinder, piston number 4 is also halfway through an upward stroke, exhaust. Between the firing of cylinders 1 and 4 cylinder number 3 will fire. Between the firing of cylinders 4 and 1 cylinder number 2 will fire. Cylinders 1 and 4 are equally spaced in the ignition cycle, therefore they would be grouped in the intake system. These tubes are designed to a length that provides the best compromise for airflow. An example of a "tuned port" intake system is the 5.0 and 5.7 liter GM engines as used in the high performance Corvettes, Camaros and Firebirds. Although there are manifolds on the market that are designed to improve the performance of these applications, the stock manifold is pretty good.

The EEC-IV (fuel injection) computer selects the intake runner set to be used. A signal is sent to a vacuum motor which will change from the use of one set of runners to the other set at about 2200 rpm.

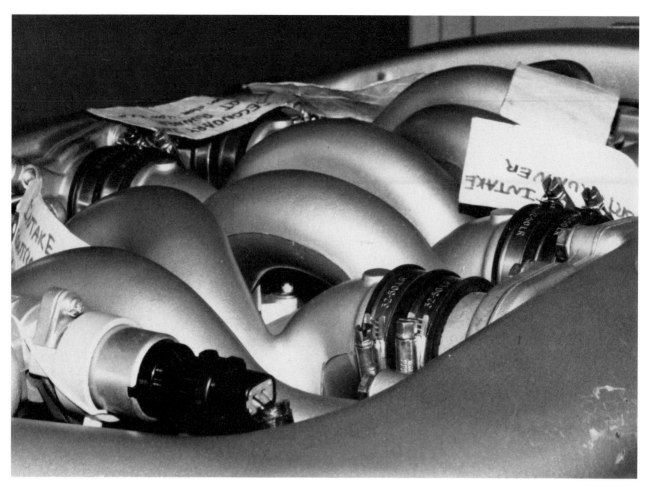

The use of two sets of runners makes the intake manifold look very complicated. My first view of the 3.0 SHO engine was followed by several nights of restless sleep with dreams of 12 cylinder Jaguar valve adjustments.

There is little that can or needs to be done to improve the intake system on the SHO engine. Routine inspection of the rubber runner to plenum couplers as well as the vacuum motor should be performed.

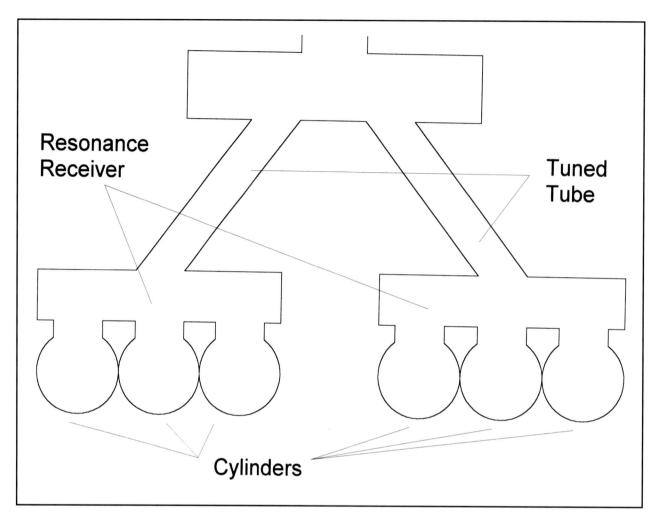

Resonance Receiver

Tuned Tube

Cylinders

The tuned tube of the 3.0 SHO and other tune port fuel injection manifolds is critical. In fixed length manifolds such as those on the 5.0 and 5.7 Chevy/Pontiac engines the engineer must predict the engine RPM and air mass/flow range the engine will be operated in. When engine modifications change the usual or critical RPM and air mass/flow range the intake manifold runners should be replaced with those designed to handle the proper mass and flow rate. Most any performance parts catalog will have several examples.

# Chapter 7

# Fuel Injection fuel pressure control

**Control**
There are a few things that need to be said about fuel pressure when talking about fuel injection systems and manifolds. When the intake manifold is modified or replaced the changes in manifold pressure that occur during different load conditions and engine speeds can affect the fuel pressure requirements.

**Fuel pressure increase on acceleration**
In theory the fuel pressure of a multipoint (injectors in the manifold) fuel injection system must allow for a fuel pressure in-

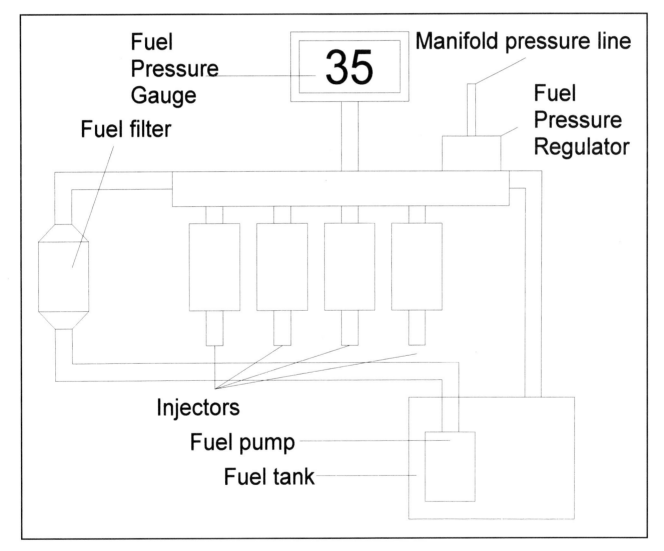

Fuel Pressure Gauge

Fuel filter

35

Manifold pressure line

Fuel Pressure Regulator

Injectors

Fuel pump

Fuel tank

Fuel pressure is critical to the proper flow rate of the fuel into the intake manifold. On mutipoint fuel injected engines there is a vacuum line between the fuel pressure regulator and the intake manifold. If the replacement manifold increases the air flow manifold pressure will increase. Replacing the stock fuel pressure regulator with one that will track the changes in manifold pressure will maximize performance. The "rising rate" fuel pressure regulators can be found for many applications in performance catalogs.

crease when the engine is under load. As previously discussed when the load on the engine increases, the pressure in the manifold also increases. This means that the pressure into which the fuel must be injected also increases. If the fuel pressure were to remain the same while the pressure in the manifold increased, the pressure differential across the tip of the injector will decrease. This means that less fuel can force its way through the injector and into the manifold, and therefore into the cylinder. For this reason multipoint injection systems have a vacuum line (or more correctly a manifold pressure line) that runs from the intake manifold to the fuel pressure regulator. The rising pressure fills a chamber behind the regulator diaphragm. As the pressure rises in this chamber it effectively increases the spring rate of the regulator, and the fuel pressure rises. Ideally, the rise in fuel pressure should approximate the rise in manifold pressure.

High flow rate manifolds, especially when accompanied by engine modifications, tend to allow a greater increase in manifold pressure earlier in the rpm curve. The rise in manifold pressure decreases the injector flow rate. The increase in manifold pressure should also cause an increase in the fuel pressure. But does the rise in fuel pressure appropriately match the rise in manifold pressure and the increased demand created by the engine modifications? Maybe yes, maybe no. What's needed is an adjustable fuel pressure regulator and a little experimenting.

## Rising rate pressure regulators

The rising rate fuel pressure regulator may be the best of the adjustable regulators. It is designed to increase the fuel pressure precisely 1/2 psi for every psi increase in manifold pressure. Standard regulators increase the fuel pressure very abruptly, typically from 35 to 45 psi at an idle, to 45-55 as soon as the throttle is opened. This means that increasing the fuel pressure on this regulator will cause rich running under certain load conditions. The rising rate regulator increases the fuel pressure gradually and steadily. This means that adjusting the fuel pressure to a higher level for better performance at a low speed should give better performance at all speeds and load conditions.

# Chapter 8

# What is Available

The content of this chapter has plagued me since the beginning of this project. On the one hand I feel obligated not to allow this chapter to read like an annotated catalogue for intake manifolds. I also did not want the material to be out of date before the books even made it to the shelves of the book stores. On the other hand, it would not be fair to take the reader through the detail up to this point and not offer information about products currently in the marketplace.

## Available manifolds

Let us begin with a list of the manufacturers. Since songs like "Surfin' Safari" and "Little Deuce Coupe" are part of my adolescence, I have to talk about Edelbrock first. This is not to imply that Edelbrock is the best or even my preference, it is just that if you can remember what you were doing when you heard about Sputnik going into orbit, then Edelbrock is synonymous with intake manifolds.

## Edelbrock

| Product name | Manifold type | Carb, TBI or PFI? | Federally legal? | California legal? |
|---|---|---|---|---|
| Performer | Street/ dual plane idle to 5000rpm | Carb | Yes | No, check with local referee |
| Performer RPM | Streetable 1500-6500rpm | Carb | Yes | No |
| Performer TBI | Street/ power replacement for trucks/vans | TBI | Yes | No |
| High flow TPI | Street/track | TPI | Yes | No |
| Torker II | Rough idle street/track 2500-6500rpm | Carb | Yes - some years, check with local authority | No |
| Victor 454-R | Track 4000-8500rpm | Carb | No | No |
| Victor 454-O | Track 3500-7500 | Carb | No | No |
| Victor 454-TD | Track 5000-9000rpm | Carb | No | No |
| Victor Jr. | Track 3500-8000rpm | Carb | No | No |
| Victor 4X4 | Track 5000-8000rpm | Carb | No | No |
| Victor-E | Track 4500-8000rpm | Carb | No | No |
| Bow-Tie II Victor Jr. | Track 3500-8000rpm | Carb | No | No |
| Victor High-Port | Track 4500-8500rpm | Carb | No | No |
| Victor High-Port Jr. | Track 4000-8000rpm | Carb | No | No |
| Victor Jr. 302 | Track 3500-8000rpm | Carb | No | No |

| Product name | Manifold type | Carb, TBI or PFI? | Federally legal? | California legal? |
|---|---|---|---|---|
| SB-Chevy Vintage Series C-26 | Streetable 2500-6500rpm | Dual Carb | Yes, some years, check with local authority | No |
| BB-Chevy Dual 4-Bbl | Streetable 2500-6500rpm | Dual Carb | Yes, some years, check with local authority | No |
| Chrysler 440 Dual 4-Bbl | Street | Dual Carb | Yes, some years, check with local authority | No |
| SB-Chevy Tri-Power | Street | Triple Carb | Yes, some years, check with local authority | No |
| Chrysler 440 Tarantula TM-7 | Track 3500-7500rpm | Carb | No | No |
| SB-Chevy Street Tunnel Ram | Streetable 3500-7500rpm | Dual Carb | Yes, some years, check with local authority | No |
| BB-Chevy Street Tunnel Ram 2-0 | Streetable 3500-7500rpm | | | |

## Weiand

| Product name | Manifold type | Carb, TBI or PFI? | Federally legal? | California legal? |
|---|---|---|---|---|
| X-CELerator Buick, GM, Jeep V-6 | Street | 4Bbl Carb 390-650cfm | Yes, some years, check with local authority | No |
| Team "G" Power Ram Buick, GM, Jeep V-6 | Streetable 2500-7500rpm | 4Bbl Carb 650-750cfm | Yes, some years, check with local authority | No |
| Action Plus SB-Chevy with EGR | Street/Track idle to 6000rpm | Carb Street: 500-650cfm Track: 650-750cfm | Yes with stock carb | Yes with stock carb |
| Action Plus SB-Chevy without EGR | Street/Track idle to 6000rpm | Carb Street: 500-650cfm Track: 650-750cfm | Yes with stock carb | Yes with stock carb |
| Action Plus SB-Chevy | Street/Track idle to 6300rpm | Carb Street: 600-750cfm Track: 650-850cfm | Yes, some years, check with local authority | No |
| Stealth SB-Chevy | Street/Track idle to 6800 | Carb Street: 600-700cfm Track: 700-800cfm | Yes, some years, check with local authority | No |
| X-CELerator SB-Chevy | Streetable 1500-6000rpm | Carb Street: 500-600cfm Track: 600-750cfm | Yes, some years, check with local authority | No |

| Product name | Manifold type | Carb, TBI or PFI? | Federally legal? | California legal? |
|---|---|---|---|---|
| X-CELerator SB-Chevy | Streetable 2000-6500rpm | Carb Street: 500-650cfm Track: 600-750cfm | Yes, some years, check with local authority | No |
| Team "G" Street Ram SB-Chevy | Street/Track 2000-6500rpm 650-750cfm Track: 750-850cfm | Carb Street: | Yes, some years, check with local authority | No |
| Team "G" Power Ram SB-Chevy | Track 2800-7200rpm | Carb Track: 650-850cfm | No | No |
| Team "G" Track Ram SB-Chevy | Track with 3/4" raised plenum 2800-7800rpm with 2" raised plenum 3000-8200 | Carb Track: 650-850cfm | No | No |
| Hi-Ram SB-Chevy | Streetable/ Track 2800-8000rpm | Carb Street: Single 4V 600-750cfm Dual 4V 390-650cfm Track: Single 4V 700-850cfm Dual 4V 600-850cfm | Yes, some years, check with local authority | No |
| Action Plus BB Chevy | Street/Track Idle-6500rpm | Carb Street: 600-750cfm Street perform: 650-750cfm Track: 700-850cfm | Yes, some years, check with local authority | No |
| X-CELerator BB-Chevy | Street/Track 1500-7000rpm | Carb Street: 600-750cfm Street Perform: 650-750cfm Track: 700-850cfm | Yes, some years, check with local authority | No |
| Stealth BB-Chevy | Street/Track Idle-7000rpm (Oval port and round port models available) | Carb Street: 650-750cfm Track: 700-850cfm | Yes, some years, check with local authority | No |
| Team "G" Track Ram BB-Chevy | Track Short: 2500-8200rpm | Carb 750-850cfm | No | No |

| | | | | |
|---|---|---|---|---|
| Team "G" 4500 BB-Chevy | Tall: 2500-8200rpm Track 2800-8500rpm | Carb Holley 4500 Dominator | No | No |
| Team "G" Track Ram BB-Chevy | Track 2500-7900rpm | Carb 750-850cfm | No | No |
| Team "G" 4500 | Track 2800-8300rpm | Carb Holley 4500 Dominator | No | No |
| Hi-Ram Single carb | Track 2500-7800rpm | Carb Street: 650-750cfm Track: 750-850cfm | No | No |
| Hi-Ram Dual Carb | Streetable/ Track 2500-7800rpm | Dual Carb Street: 650-750cfm Track: 750-850cfm | Yes, some years, check with local authority | No |
| Pro Hi-Ram Dual Carb | Streetable/ Track 3600-9000rpm | Dual Carb Street: 650-750cfm Track: 750-850cfm | Yes, some years, check with local authority | No |
| Pro Hi Ram 4500 | Track 3600-9500rpm | Carb Holley 4500 Dominator | No | No |
| Super Pro Hi-Ram | Track 3000-10,000rpm | Dual Carb 700-850cfm | No | No |
| Super Pro Hi-Ram 4500 | Track 3000-10,000rpm | Dual Carb Holley 4500 Dominator | No | No |
| Super Pro Hi-Ram Fuel Injection | Track 3000-10,000rpm | Fuel Injection Enderle or Hilborn also uses 6-71 supercharger | No | No |

The above list for Weiand products covers intake manifolds available for Chevy applications. There are similar manifolds available for Ford and Chrysler applications.

**World Products**

| Product name | Manifold type | Carb, TBI or PFI? | Federally legal? | California legal? |
|---|---|---|---|---|
| Sportsman Intake Manifold | Street/track 1500-6500rpm | Carb | Yes, some years, check with local authority | No |

**Holley**

| Product name | Manifold type | Carb, TBI or PFI? | Federally legal? | California legal? |
|---|---|---|---|---|
| Street Dominator | Street performance Idle-6000rpm | Carb | Yes | Yes |
| Chevrolet 396-454ci Big-Block V-8 | Street performance Idle-5200rpm | Carb | Yes, some years, check with local authority | No |
| Chevrolet 262-400ci Small-Block | Street performance Idle-7200rpm | Carb | Yes, some years, check with local authority | No |
| Ford 221, 260, 289, 302ci t (Excep Boss) V-8 | Street performance 1200-4800rpm | Carb | Yes, some years, check with local authority | No |
| AMC (1970-79 304-401ci V-8) | Street performance Idle-4800rpm | Carb | Yes, some years, check with local authority | No |
| Buick (1982-86 2.5L) 4 cyl | Street performance Idle-6000cfm | Carb | Yes, some years, check with local authority | No |
| Buick (1975-79 231ci V-6 1980 and later | Street performance Idle-4500rpm | Carb | Yes, some years, check with local authority | No |
| Chevrolet 4 cylinder (1982-86 2.5L) | Street performance Idle-6000rpm | Stock Throttle Body Injection | Yes | No |
| Chevrolet (1978-80 200, 229ci V-6) | Street performance Idle-4500rpm | Carb 450cfm | Yes, some years, check with local authority | No |
| Chevrolet Big-Block V-8 (396-454) | Street performance Idle-4800rpm | Carb | Yes, some years, check with local authority | Yes, some years, check with local authority |
| Chevrolet Small block V-8 1973-86 262-350-400ci 1987 and later with aluminum heads | Street performance Idle-4800rpm | Carb | Yes, some years, check with local authority | No |
| Chevrolet Big ) Block V-8 (396-454) | Street performance Idle-4800rpm | Carb | Yes, some years, check with local authority | Yes, some years, check with local authority |
| Pontiac (1980 231ci V-6) | Street performance Idle-4500rpm | Carb | Yes, some years, check with local | No |
| Chevrolet Small block (283-400ci V-8) | Track 4500-7600rpm | Carb | No | No |
| Chevrolet Big block (396-454ci V-8) | Track 4500-8500rpm | Carb | No | No |
| Chrysler Small block V-8 | Track 4500-8500rpm | Carb | No | No |

| Product name | Manifold type | Carb, TBI or PFI? | Federally legal? | California legal? |
| --- | --- | --- | --- | --- |
| (273-360ci) Chevrolet Small block | Track 4500-8500rpm | Dual Carb | No | No |
| (283-400ci V-8) Chevrolet Big block | Track 4500-8500rpm | Dual Carb | No | No |
| (396-454ci V-8) Chrysler Small block V-8 (273-360ci) | Track 4500-8500rpm | Dual Carb | No | No |

**Offenhauser**

| Product name | Manifold type | Carb, TBI or PFI? | Federally legal? | California legal? |
| --- | --- | --- | --- | --- |
| Ford 429-460 Port-O-Sonic | Track 3500-8500rpm | Carb | No | No |
| Ford 240-300 Inline 6 cylinder | Street Performance 1000-5000rpm | Carb | Yes, some years, check with local authority | No |

California legal

| Product name | Manifold type | Carb, TBI or PFI? | Federally legal? | California legal? |
| --- | --- | --- | --- | --- |
| Weiand Automotive Industrial Model 8000 | Street Performance | Carb | Yes, some years, check with local authority | Yes, some years, check with local authority |
| Chevrolet Big Block V-8 (396-454) | Street Performance Idle-4800rpm | Carb | Yes, some years, check with local authority | Yes, some years, check with local authority |

Many years ago a friend of mine and I built a race car. That is to say we assembled a facsimile of a race car. We spared no expense, with an engineering budget of $1000 and an annual budget of over $500 we built a 1965 Ford Mustang and went racing. We went to the local auto supply store and paid $100 for a set of headers (other than the intake manifold this was the single biggest investment we made in the whole car.) Now, the rules for road racing required that the exhaust system exit from under the car behind the driver. The headers, of course exited in the engine compartment. In shopping around we found that most custom exhaust shops wanted more than $100 to build an appropriate set of pipes! After much discussion and brainstorming, my partner and I went to the local hardware store and bought stove pipe. We then hung the pipe from the chassis of the car and sealed the seams with muffler tape. My partner, being a bit of a fuddy-duddy, was concerned that the tech inspectors might not see the humor in the use of stove pipe as exhaust pipe. I agreed that the tech inspectors had no sense of humor. The next step, therefore, was to wrap the end of the headers and the stove pipe with a heat-resistant "plaster" wrap.

A few days later it was time for tech inspection. As we pushed the car closer to the inspectors, one of them recognized us as the ones who had been there the month before with a cookie sheet being used as a carburetor overflow guard. He raised an eyebrow. I tried to look unfamiliar to him. He frowned.

"Well what bit of originality do you have for me this month," he said as though he dreaded to ask.

"Nothing," I replied.

Everything went well until he got down on his hands and knees to look at the exhaust system. "What in the name of Andy Granatelli is that?"

By this time my quick thinking partner had arrived. "That is chrome-moly 0.80 mil wall with a thermoplastic infusion layer."

The tech inspector looked at my partner; he looked at the stunned expression on my face; my partner looked at the tech inspector. The poor guy knew that it was stove pipe covered in plaster but my partner's line of bovine excrement was so good that he could only nod, "Okay."

Now here we are 20 years later, and that very concept is being put to use in many forms of racing. I wonder, could that tech inspector have stolen my partner's idea and gotten rich?

# Chapter 9
# Exhaust Theory

The purpose of the exhaust system is to provide an efficient way to guide the exhaust gases from the engine and as quietly as possible deposit them into the atmosphere. For decades the exhaust system really was little more than this. In the mid-seventies, however, the Environmental Protection Agency established guidelines that required the manufacturers to install a chemical catalyst in the exhaust system. This catalyst was intended to convert two chemicals into two other chemicals. This "catalytic converter" will be discussed in detail later. For now, if the car came equipped with a catalytic converter, it *must* remain installed if the vehicle is to be driven on the street.

**The Stock Exhaust System**

In the stock exhaust system there will be an exhaust manifold attached to the head. This manifold is generally made of cast iron. Historically, little if any attention was paid to maximizing exhaust gas flow. The manufacturers tended to design the exhaust manifold just for its fundamental purpose of carrying exhaust gases away from the cylinder head. In the mid-seventies the manufacturers were faced with Federal mandates to reduce oxides of nitrogen emissions. These emissions occur when the temperature of combustion exceeds 2500 degrees F.

Several things were done to ensure that combustion temperatures remained below 2500 degrees F as often as possible while the engine was running. Among these things was a reduction in the compression ratio. Reducing the compression ratio to reduce oxides of nitrogen has a couple of negative side effects. First, the fuel economy suffers severely. On many occasions I have heard

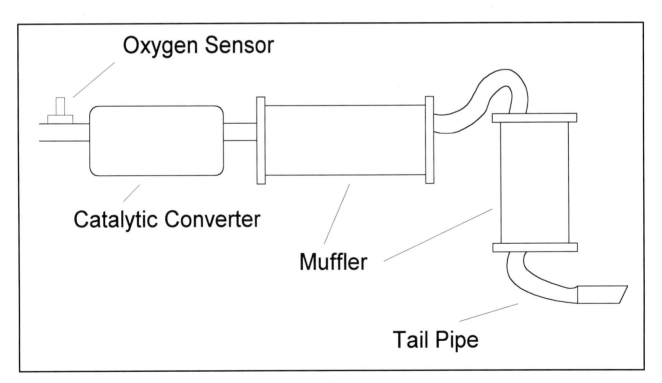

There is an old saying, "They don't make them like they used to." When it comes to the stock exhaust system we can be glad. In the old days of chrome and fins you bought a new car knowing that you would have to replace the exhaust system several times. New alloys and new coatings make exhaust replacement rare enough to encourage exhaust specialty shops to expand into brakes and tuneups.

Exhaust headers were first brought into the performance market to satisfy the needs of racing. The design was basically steel tubes welded to a flange that bolted to the cylinder head. This design was brought into the stock engine during the 1980's. Some of the applications to use these steel manifolds were as unostentatious as a 2.5 liter Citation.

If the engine you are modifying is of a vintage later than the early eighties and if that vehicle is destined to be used on the street, be sure there are provisions for the oxygen sensor. Of course if you are in a California or similar jurisdiction the legal replacement exhaust will be California Air Resources Board approved and therefore have provisions for any required exhaust gas oxygen sensor.

owners' anecdotes about owning a 1974 vehicle and getting 20-25mpg and also owning a virtually identical 1975 model and getting half the mileage.

Second, and to many more importantly, the power output of the engine drops considerably. As a result of this power loss the manufacturers began to look for ways to get the power output of the engine back up. For the first time in decades the car manufacturers began to explore alternate designs. In some applications the exhaust manifold has evolved into something that closely resembles a "header" system.

From the exhaust manifold the exhaust gases travel to the front exhaust pipe. It is either in the exhaust manifold or in this front exhaust pipe or "down pipe" that the oxygen sensor is located. If the vehicle came from the factory equipped with an oxygen sensor, the oxygen sensor *must* be retained in its original position relative to the cylinder head after any modifications. Locating the oxygen sensor too far from the cylinder head will cause it to be slow to warm up. If the oxygen sensor takes too long to reach operating temperature, the emissions will be affected. There will be excessive emissions while the computer is waiting for the oxygen sensor to reach operating temperature. If the oxygen sensor is located too close to the cylinder head it may get too hot and be damaged.

The front exhaust pipe is connected to the catalytic converter. Since the introduction of the catalytic converter in 1975, performance enthusiasts and the public in general has seen fit to remove it. It is generally believed that the converter restricts the exhaust system. Very clever methods were devised to eliminate the converter. In the early days a technician would suspect a restricted or damaged converter and install a "test pipe" and conveniently forget to

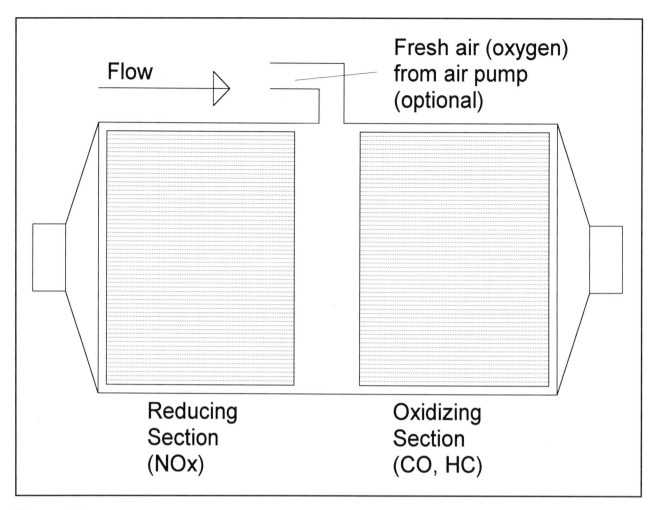

Flow

Fresh air (oxygen) from air pump (optional)

Reducing Section (NOx)

Oxidizing Section (CO, HC)

The catalytic converter most commonly used today consists of two sections. The reducing section is upstream in the exhaust flow. The job of the reducing section is to strip oxygen from the oxides of nitrogen. This will yield nitrogen and oxygen. Both of these gases are normal, harmless atmospheric gases. Next comes the oxidizing section. The job of the oxidizing section is to add oxygen to the exhaust gases, converting carbon monoxide into carbon dioxide as well as converting raw hydrocarbons into carbon dioxide and water.

was better. And in some ways it was. Decades before the introduction of the portable CD player, a loud exhaust system was a blessing to the audiophile who would otherwise be forced to listen to an eight-track.

**Scavenging**

Another important job of the exhaust system is to help scavenge the post-combustion gases from the combustion chamber. Each of the exhaust manifold runners carries exhaust gases in turn to the ex-

haust down pipe. As each cylinder sends its gases through the manifold, they pass across the tubes in the manifold that lead to the other cylinders. The movement of the gases across these "empty" tubes creates a low pressure area. Additionally, the velocity of the gases is maintained in the exhaust pipe after the exhaust valve opens and as the next exhaust valve opens. When the next exhaust valve opens, it opens into the previously mentioned low pressure area. The gases in the combustion chamber

immediately begin to accelerate. The acceleration assists the piston in clearing the combustion chamber. You may be thinking by this time about what happens when the gases enter the low pressure area and cause the low pressure to become a high pressure. That is where the velocity of the gases from the preceding cylinder come into play. The inertia of those gases helps to drag the gases from the cylinder with the open valve along the exhaust pipe. This is called scavenging. Each cylinder's ex-

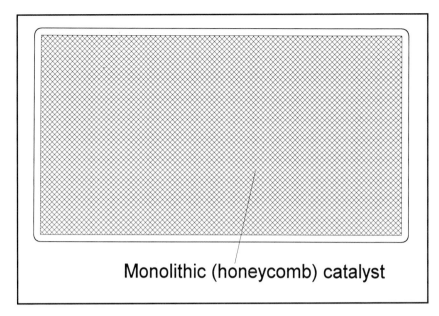

Monolithic (honeycomb) catalyst

The catalytic converter was introduced in the mid-1970's. It has a reputation for decreasing engine performance. When the engine is tweaked to its maximum that may be true. However, for the common street machine the frontal cross-section of the converter is quite adequate.

haust gases act the same way in turn on each of the next cylinders.

## Backpressure

Backpressure has long been a nasty word to the performance enthusiast. After all, if the engine cannot exhale it cannot inhale, and if it cannot inhale it cannot create power. In the past many "racers" have gone to extremes in reducing exhaust back pressure. At many of the dirt 1/4mi track in the south of the sixties and seventies it was very common to see low budget racers eliminating back pressure altogether by letting the exhaust gases simply exit the cylinder head. On the surface this might seem quite logical...but what about scavenging? Simply, the advantages of scavenging almost always exceed the disadvantage

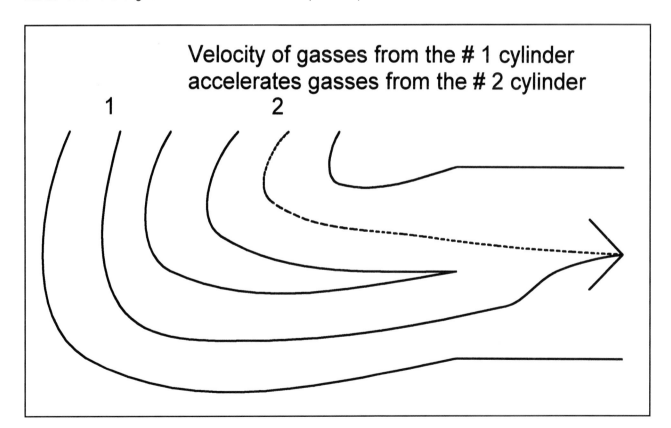

# Velocity of gasses from the # 1 cylinder accelerates gasses from the # 2 cylinder

In addition to providing a path for the exhaust gases to exit harmlessly away from the vehicle, the exhaust system also helps the engine breath. Each consecutive cylinder helps to accellerate the exaust gases from the preceding cylinder. This forms a slight vacuum in the preceding exhaust runner which reduces the resistance to flow in the exhaust system.

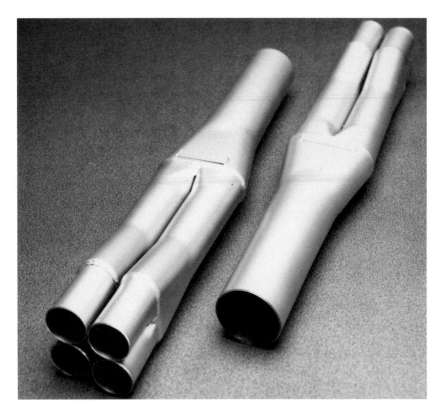

Many performance exhaust component manufacturers build scavenging header collectors. These collectors increase the exhaust flow rate by creating low pressure areas in each of the header pipes leading from the exhaust ports of the cylinder head.

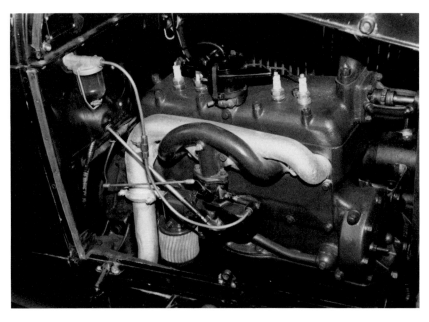

In the distant past very little attention was paid to the performance of the exhaust system. This Model A engine could have benefited from the improvements offered by a modern exhaust system. Of course the stock exhaust system matches the needs of the engine.

remove and install a new converter. This is highly illegal. Another, even more clever meth-od, was to remove the converter, break up the catalyst, dump the catalyst and reinstall the hollow converter. This, too, is a serious violation of EPA regulations.

The reality of the catalytic converter is that they often have a cross-section many times greater than the cross-section of the rest of the exhaust system. In reality a catalytic converter in good condition has sufficient flow capability for virtually any streetable modifications. There will more about catalytic converters in subsequent chapters.

The next component is the front connector pipe. This pipe connects the catalytic converter to the first of two possible mufflers. Of all the components in the exhaust system it is the mufflers that provide the greatest potential restriction and the greatest potential for improved components.

## Purpose of the exhaust system

Perhaps the most important function of the exhaust system is to route the noxious and poisonous fumes from the engine safely away from the passenger compartment. Federal, state and local ordinances also require that sound levels be reduced by the exhaust system. Shortly after I met my wife (we were both in high school at the time), I bought a Fiat 850 Coupe. This "race car" was attractive to me primarily because of its Abarth exhaust system. I soon found out that this was not a good car for sneaking around in. Without a doubt, it was identifiable to every future father-in-law, brother-in-law and police officer in Fort Worth. Officer Terry was my high school nemesis. Looking back, there is little doubt in my mind that he would hear me coming, finish his lunch, pick up his radar gun and try to nail me. In those days we all believed that loud

# Chapter 10
## Stock

The range of stock exhaust systems goes all the way from a series of pipes whose sole function is to keep the occupants of the car from becoming asphyxiated or poisoned by carbon monoxide, to highly researched performance exhaust systems. It may surprise you to know that many of the more thoroughly thought out exhaust systems are found on applications usually thought of as a modest commuter rig. Many of these commuter vehicles are designed to maximize fuel economy; maximizing fuel economy is actually a performance issue. When the exhaust system flows well, less energy is used to help the engine breath, and more energy is used to push the car down the road. When the energy used to flow the exhaust gases is minimized and the power used to

push the car down the road is maximized, the fuel economy improves.

Now that I have said all this, I should point out that I realize you have not read this book to this point to find out how to get 100 miles per gallon (mpg). Let us talk about fire-spouting power.

### The manifold

Today's stock exhaust manifolds reflect the technology of the decade in which the engine was designed. In 1957 who would have dreamed that in 1994 we would still be driving around with engines that were designed while the Edsel was still on the drawing board? I know, every time I am bold enough to make this statement someone always says, "Wait a minute, the P-309

5.1 liter V-10 is a brand new design." Well let us see: overhead valve "V" layout with the chain driven camshaft located above the crankshaft, cross-flow heads and hydraulic lifters operating tubular push-rods. Sounds very similar to a 409 to me.

These older design engines—the 312, the 409 and their children—use an exhaust manifold virtually unchanged in concept since the decade of the ducktail. The cast iron manifold offers low cost, good durability and reasonably good flow. In applications where they are exposed to limited cooling from outside air and are subjected to vibration, there are cracking problems.

In most cases the cast iron manifold consists of a tube running the length of the cylinder head with the front exhaust pipe connected at some point. Inherent to this design is the fact that exhaust gas velocity remains quite low and therefore scavenging is kept to a minimum. The best thing that can usually be done with these manifolds is to find a door that needs to be held open and put them to work doing something they are good at.

In the seventies and especially in the eighties many applications began to use tube steel manifolds. These offered greater flexibility in design, greater immunity to cracking, and a "cooler" look. Rather than each exhaust port in the cylinder head feeding into a short tube that runs immediately into a common tube, these tube steel manifolds allowed the designer to make long runs to the collection point. The longer runs provided for greater exhaust gas velocities and therefore better scavenging.

This Model T engine shows an exhaust manifold typical of the stock exhaust manifolds used right up to the 1990's. (Note the ignition system. Who said that distributorless ignition is one of the byproducts of the emission control age?)

As much as we like to think that automotive technology has come a long way since the 1950's it is sobering to realize that most of the larger engines in use as we entered the 1990's were clones of designs that were new when this tray held a cheesburger and cherry-lime at Mel's drive-in.

## The pipes

I have the greatest admiration for those courageous men at Midas. It is a little known fact that when certain alloys oxidize they develop an affinity for saline solutions. As a result any rust that falls from the exhaust system while changing or working with the pipes or muffler will plot a deliberate vector for you eyes. Additionally, can you imagine spending your entire life with rust flakes between your teeth?

## Design
### Single Wall

The single wall pipe has been the standard of the industry for decades. Back in the days of Eisenhower and "the good life" you could plan on replacing these pipes frequently—in some climates annually. Since the fifties the manufacturers and exhaust system suppliers have done many things to improve the life expectancy of these pipes. Today companies that grew to national size very quickly in the post-war years working exclusively on exhaust systems have had to branch out into other areas of auto repair. This is due in no small measure to the increase in exhaust pipe quality and the decrease in rust.

Today's exhaust pipes feature coatings that reduce rust and corrosion to the point where it is virtually non-existent. My dad bought a new 1970 Buick Skylark and, as had been his practice since before the Korean conflict, immediately made an appointment for exhaust work a year later. The year passed; he had to cancel the appointment. Another year, another year, and when the car was traded in 1978, it still had the original exhaust system. Now if the reader is surprised by the fact that Paul McCartney was in a rock band before Wings, you might wonder why we found this durability to be amazing. On the other hand if you remember being touched when The Big Bopper, Richie Valens, and Buddy Holly died, you know why this was amazing.

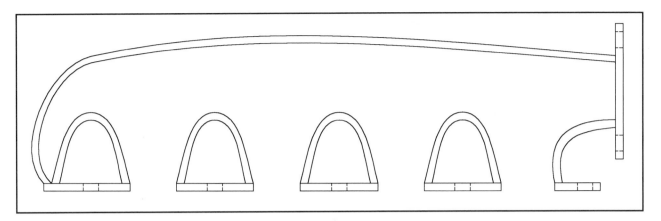

The typical stock exhaust manifold has changed very little since the Doughboy's returned from France. It is merely a cast iron gathering place for exhaust gases. The benefits of scavenging are utilized poorly at best.

## Dual Wall

Reduced performance as a result of exhaust restrictions is not unique to performance applications. In the early seventies we began to have cars coming in to the department store auto service center where I worked, complaining about reduced power.

The answer was always a tune up. Unfortunately this answer was not always right. When we checked the exhaust system, we assumed that if the pipe looked good on the outside then it did not have a rust problem. Unfortunately we did not, at first, know about dual wall pipes. On these pipes it was not uncommon for the inner pipe to rust and partially collapse, restricting exhaust flow.

The good part about dual wall pipes is that it gave me another use for my favorite diagnostic tool—a hammer. If, when the pipe was tapped on, you could hear rust falling on the inside, then you knew that the lack of power was probably associated with a collapsed inner pipe.

The whole exhaust system is thought of as a restriction to the flow of exhaust gases and is therefore considered to impede performance. There is no doubt that on many applications, and after engine modifications have been performed, the exhaust system may indeed impede flow. Before spending a lot of money on "trick" exhaust systems, however, keep in mind that the total volume of the mufflers is many times greater than the displacement of the engine. In fact, typically, the front muffler has 4-10 times the swept volume of the engine, while the rear muffler has 3-8 times. This implies that if back pressure is occurring in an engine, it is not because of restriction but because of resonance waves. The "biggest" exhaust system, therefore, may not be the "best" exhaust system.

The exhaust system of this old Buick shows some of the modern concepts of exhaust designs. Note that the exhaust manifold is located above the intake manifold, heat therefore is not transferred readily from the exhaust to the intake. The upswept design of the manifold take advantage of the fact that the warm exhaust gases should rise. The angle of the exhaust runners where they attach to the head increases scavenging.

Heat resistant wrap on the exhaust headers will reduce the underhood temperature. Since in most performance modified setups the intake draws its air from under the hood high underhood temperatures can severely reduce performance.

## Heat Resistant Wrap

If I had been born a half a generation earlier, I am sure I would have been one of those obnoxious kids that would call the corner drug store and ask, "Do you have Prince Albert in a can?" And if the reply was, "Yes," then I would have said, "Well you better let him out." Now if you do not understand that joke it is because you were born a half generation or more after me. I love to go into "speed shops" and ask the benefits of different products they have in the store. For instance, a few years back, a heat absorbing exhaust wrap became available. You would not believe some of the answers I have gotten concerning its benefits. "It protects the plug wires." "It protects the electronics." I could go on. Reduced underhood temperatures do help to prolong the life of, and thus "protect," plug wires and electronic gear. An additional benefit is that maintaining a high temperature in the exhaust gases reduces the drop in their velocity as they pass through the system, thus increasing the scavenging effect. As a youth of the sixties who is receiving counseling because he was unable to drive a new Chevelle SS 396 to school like the other kids, the performance use of this product is to reduce underhood temperatures to ensure a denser air mass for the intake system.

Many performance cars use an air cleaner designed to pick up air from under the hood. In the winter in Fairbanks, Alaska, that is probably a good idea. But in Tucson the underhood temperature, just caused by the radiant heat of the engine, will be extremely high. Add to that the radiant heat from the exhaust and the air temperature can easily be as high as when under high levels of boost. These exhaust wrap-

The catalytic converter is the most obvious emission control device on the modern automobile. No matter how much anyone might wish that they could eliminate the converter, it is required by Federal law, there is no jurisdiction in the United States or Canada that will permit its removal on a street vehicle.

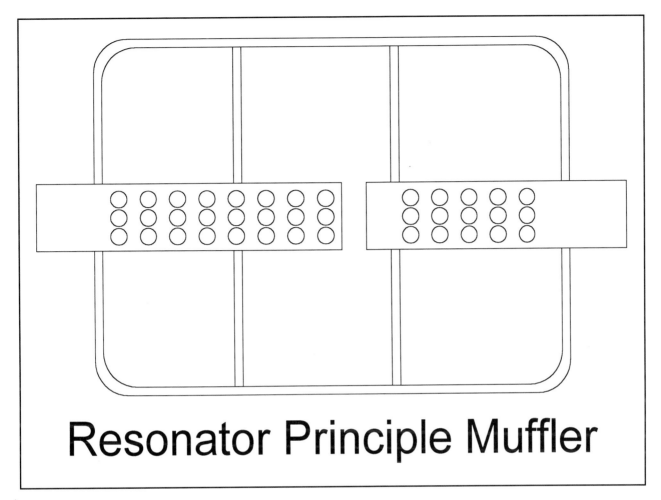

# Resonator Principle Muffler

The resonator decreases exhaust noise by splitting the sound into a number of frequencies. The holes shown in the entry and exit tubes of the resonator each divide out different frequencies. In some performance mufflers these holes are designed to produce only a series of tones selected for a throaty sound.

ping products reduce the underhood temperatures, allowing the intake system to utilize cooler, denser air. The denser the air going into the intake the more horsepower the air will yield.

## Catalytic Converter

When the catalytic converter was introduced in 1975 it meant the beginning of the end for leaded gasoline. These early oxidizing catalytic converters consisted of a platinum/palladium coating over an aluminum oxide substrate. The platinum was not compatible with teraethyl lead, requiring that it not be present in the fuel used in catalyst equipped vehicles. The job of the catalyst is to provide an environment where enough heat can be generated to allow further combustion of the HC and CO to occur. The heating of the catalytic converter begins with the hot exhaust gases. When the converter is warm enough it begins to combine CO with $O_2$ to create $CO_2$. This chemical reaction in turn produces more heat. The minimum operating, or "light-off", temperature of the converter is about 600 degrees F, with an optimum operating temperature of about 1200 to 1400 degrees. At a temperature of approximately 1800 degrees, the substrate will begin to melt. This means the range of temperatures at which the catalytic converter can properly operate is very narrow. Excessive temperatures can be reached when the engine runs too rich or is misfiring.

A few years ago I attended a meeting of the Society of Automotive Engineers where a representative of a company that built the converter substrates stated that a 25 percent misfire (one cylinder on a four cylinder engine) for 15 minutes was enough to begin an irreversible self de-

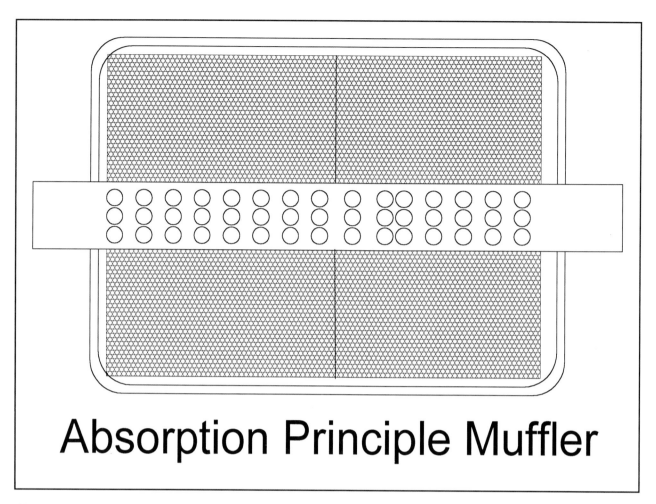

# Absorption Principle Muffler

Absorption mufflers have a tube with holes. These holes allow the accoustic vibrations to be divided in a vibration absorbing material.

struction process in the converter. This type of catalytic converter requires plenty of oxygen to do its job. This means that the exhaust gases passing through it must be the result of an air/fuel ratio of 14.7:1 or leaner.

Oxides of nitrogen are created in the combustion chamber

Glass packs were for many years considered the exhaust muffler of choice by motorheads. While they did offer improved performance over stock exhaust systems, there are many far better alternatives today.

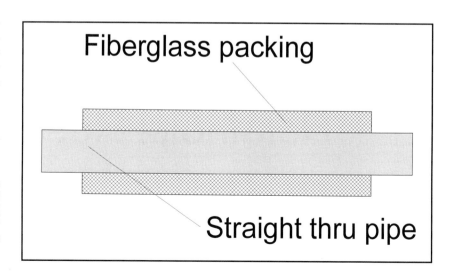

Fiberglass packing

Straight thru pipe

anytime the combustion temperature excedes 2500 degrees F. Between 1978 and 1982 there was a gradual introduction of the dual bed converter. This converter adds a second, rhodium catalyst known as the reducing section ahead of the oxidizing section. The rhodium coats an aluminum oxide substrate and reacts with the NOx passing through it. When heated to more than 600 degrees F, the nitrogen and oxygen elements of the NOx passing through it will be stripped apart. Although only about 70 to 80 percent efficient,

when coupled with the EGR valve it does a dramatic job of reducing NOx. Since the job of the reducing catalyst is to strip oxygen away from nitrogen, it works best when the exhaust gases passing though it are the result of an oxygen-poor air/fuel ratio of 14.7:1 or richer.

The only air/fuel ratio that will permit both sections of the converter to operate efficiently is an air fuel ratio of 14.7:1. The job of the oxygen feedback fuel injection systems being used today is to control the air/fuel ratio at 14.7:1 as often as possible.

On many applications, the air from the air pump, after completing its role of preheating the catalytic converter, will be directed between the front reducing section and the rear oxidizing section of the converter. This is to supply extra oxygen to improve the efficiency of the oxidizer.

## Resonators

There are many types of mufflers in use today. These range from simple resonance chambers to highly sophisticated electronic devices. To paraphrase the *Bosch Automotive*

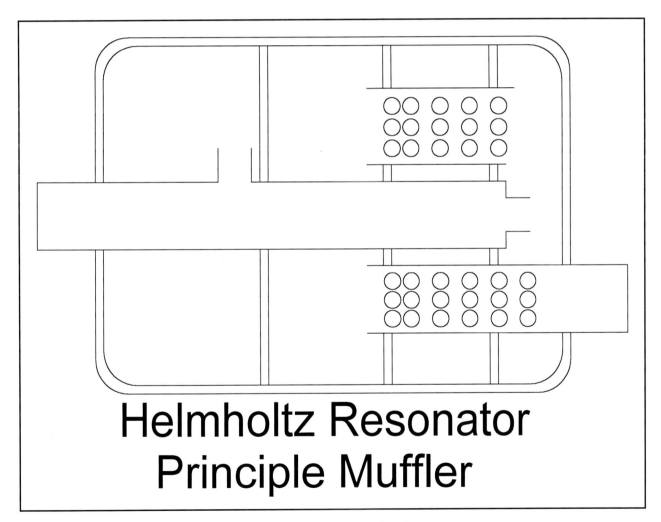

# Helmholtz Resonator Principle Muffler

The Helmholtz resonator is based on a mathematical theory of the motion of air at the end of an organ pipe which was proposed by Hermann Ludwig Ferdinand Von Helmholtz in 1859. Essentially what he said was that if you move air to the end of the tube the reaction of the air in the end of the tube will amplify some frequencies of sound when dampening others.

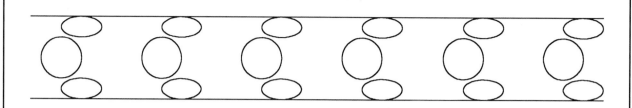

# Reflection
# Orifices

Reflection orifices are a pipe traveling through a series of chambers. In each chamber the pipe has been perforated with a series of holes. Entering from the other end of the series of chambers of a second pipe, also perforated with a series of holes. Since the holes occur at different lengths along the two pipes they will filter out different frequencies.

*Handbook*, "the resonance chamber, or resonator operates by reflecting sound back toward the sound source and by multiplying the number of sound emission points." There are tubes with small holes, or slits, in the resonator. These holes break the sound up into smaller units. While each of the smaller units individually has the same decibel potential as the exhaust gases coming down the exhaust pipe from the cylinder head, the fact that they are smaller allows the sound to dissipate more readily and therefore a quieter exhaust is achieved. In effect, it is easier to deaden a bunch of little sounds than it is to deaden one big sound.

Forcing the "big" sound to break up into a bunch of little ones requires energy. This energy must come from the exhaust gases themselves, and since the energy in the exhaust gases originates with the engine, resonators do affect the power output of the engine.

Additionally, the resonator will usually contain 2 to 7 "acoustic elements." Acoustic elements are abrupt changes in pipe cross-section or direction. Anytime the exhaust gases are forced through a smaller cross section, it requires energy. The ultimate source for this energy is the engine. Also, a change in direction means that kinetic energy must overcome inertia, and more power is lost.

The location of the resonator is critical both to the way sound is dampened and to the amount of energy the resonator diverts from pushing the car down the road. In the resonator exhaust gases are forced against the outer walls. When the resonator is located close to the engine this will result in the loss of a great deal of heat energy and therefore a loss of power. This heat loss results from the surface area of the resonator being greater than the surface area of the pipe that would otherwise be in that posi-

tion. The increased surface area dissipates the heat in the same way a radiator dissipates heat. Anytime heat energy is removed from the power train power is lost. Additionally, the outside of the resonator can become extremely hot. Depending on location, this heat can be transferred to the underbody and eventually to the passenger compartment. Many resonators feature a double outer wall with insulating material between to reduce the transfer of heat to the outside of the resonator.

If the resonator is located near the end of the exhaust system (as in the aforementioned Fiat) it is less effective in deadening the sound of the exhaust. When located at the rear of the car, the sound deadening ability will be greatly affected by the length of the tailpipe. Therefore, if the purpose of the exhaust system modification is strictly to sound "cool," (which *is* an honorable desire) then a single res-

112

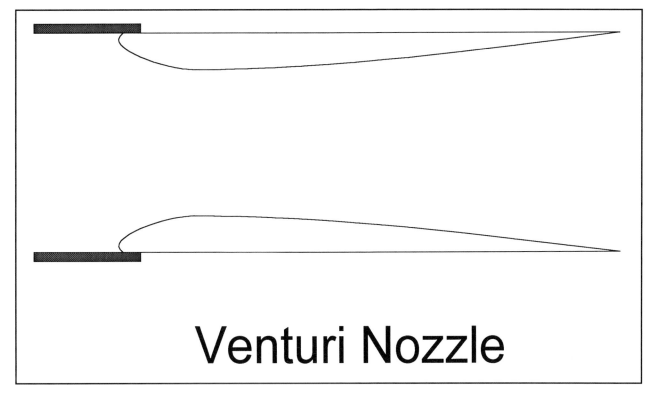

# Venturi Nozzle

A venturi nozzle is a narrowing of the pipe used to filter out the offensive frequencies.

onator at the end of the exhaust system with a selection of various length tailpipes would allow you to tune the sound of your exhaust to match the occasion. A short tailpipe to "impress" your girlfriend with the throatiness of your rod, and a long tailpipe with which to depart the wedding ceremony.

### The Absorption Muffler

Absorption mufflers use a sound deadening material to reduce engine noise. The desire of every teenage male during the sixties who did not have a pocket protector, a loop on the back of his shirt, or a slide rule on his hip was to have a set of "glass-packs" on his car. Imagine this, a 1959 Plymouth Belvedere with push button automatic, a smoking V-8 and a 17 year old at the wheel, a car so fine that when

the owner visited used car lots he would leave the keys in the door in hopes they would sell it. Yet, add a set of glass-packs and the car was magically transformed into something they would have to ban at Indy out of fairness to the competition.

"Glass pack" absorption mufflers were considered for a long time to be the ultimate in performance exhaust mufflers. Essentially, the exhaust is directed through a pipe in the muffler with a series of holes in it. The exhaust gases are directed through the holes into a heat-resistant dampening material, such as basalt wool. The advantage of this type of muffler is that it permits the exhaust gases a straight path through the muffler. The absence of bends and turns would logically reduce the back pressure in the exhaust and increase power. Unfortu-

nately we still do not live in that ideal world discussed in previous chapters. As the gases pass across the holes in the tube, the holes set up eddy currents in the gases. These eddy currents tend to impede the flow of the exhaust gases. A well thought out muffler will reduce the resistance to gas flow by carefully spacing the holes.

### Acoustic tuning, noise dampening principles
### Pipes perforated with holes

Actually this principle has been discussed already. Although a physicist would probably disagree with this analogy, the principle is as follows: Think about the flute carried by Kwai Chang Caine of the old "Kung Fu" television series. This flute was basically a bamboo tube with several holes drilled in it. Each of the holes is placed at a different

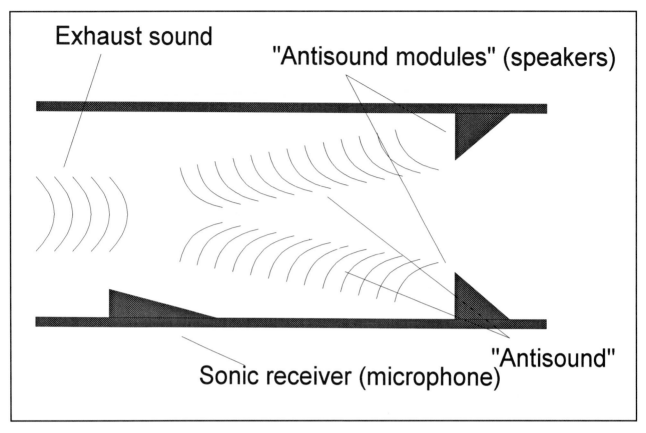

Exhaust sound

"Antisound modules" (speakers)

"Antisound"

Sonic receiver (microphone)

A new technology called an electronic muffler is making its way into the automotive industry. Although mostly experimental a sonic detector (microphone) is placed at a strategic location in the exhaust system. This microphone picks up the sound of the exhaust as it travels from the engine. An electronic circuit reproduces what amount to the photographic negative of the sound sending it out through a specially designed speaker to cancel or negate the sound of the exhaust.

length from the end of the tube. When Caine blew through the end of the tube with all the holes uncovered, a tone was generated. As he progressively placed his fingers over the open holes the sound frequency would increase. In the perforated pipe acoustic exhaust tuning system there are a series of holes located along the length of the pipe. These holes filter out and dissipate the various frequencies that make up the aggregate sound that comes through the exhaust ports of the cylinder head. These holes also form sound emission points which tend to cancel one another. To put it a little more directly, a perforated pipe takes one big sound and makes a bunch of little sounds out of it.

### Helmholtz resonator (ladder filter)

The Helmholtz resonator is based on a mathematical theory of the motion of air at the end of an organ pipe which was proposed by Hermann Ludwig Ferdinand Von Helmholtz in 1859. Essentially what he said was that if you move air to the end of the tube, the reaction of the air in the end of the tube will amplify some frequencies of sound while dampening others. Helmholtz resonators are therefore used within an exhaust system to subdue frequencies within the range of hearing while actually increasing non-offensive frequencies outside the range of human hearing, or those deemed desirable by pubescent males.

### Reflection orifices

Imagine a pipe passing through a series of chambers. In each chamber the pipe has been perforated with a series of holes. Entering from the other end of the series of chambers is a second pipe, also perforated with a series of holes. Since the holes occur at different lengths along the two pipes, they will filter out different frequencies. The ends of the chambers act as baffles to further reduce the sound of the exhaust.

114

This type of muffler, though popular for many decades, tends to be extremely heavy and cause a great deal of back pressure.

## Venturi nozzles

A venturi nozzle is simply a narrowing of the pipe use to decrease the intensity of low frequency sounds. This is usually a restriction to gas flow.

## Electronic Mufflers

This is something new and potentially very exciting. Imagine a 600hp, fire breathing monster machine so quiet you can enjoy your favorite Chopin piece while tearing up the quarter mile! Imagine a virtually silent exhaust system with virtually no restriction. This is the promise of the electronic muffler.

### Theory of sound cancellation

My wife is an ardent "Star Trek" fan. Now don't get me wrong, she does not spend her summers at Klingon Camps or thousands of dollars on authentic Star Fleet uniforms, but it is a major topic around our house. In the Star Trek television series, there is a great deal of discussion about anti-matter. It seems that, according to Mr. Spock, if two identical pieces of anti-matter were to come in contact with one another it could result in a universe-ending reaction. The electronic muffler creates anti-sound to cancel exhaust noise.

### How it operates

A sonic detector (microphone) is placed at a strategic location in the exhaust system. This microphone picks up the sound of the exhaust as it travels from the engine. An electronic circuit reproduces what amounts to a negative of that sound, sending it out through a specially designed speaker to cancel or negate the sound of the exhaust.

### What are the advantages

The main advantage is that a perfectly free-flowing exhaust system can be designed. Without baffles, resonators, perforated pipes, or any other restriction, maximum performance could be achieved with a minimum of noise. Also, the electronics could be adjusted to make your CHEvette sound like a CORvette.

# Chapter 11
## Performance

Probably the area of greatest flexibility in performance modification, without violating an emission law, is the exhaust system. There are a couple of areas that are inflexible for street performance, but for the track the possibilities are wide open.

Take a time leap with me back to 1939. The place is Tampa, Florida, at the state fair grounds. The popular racing engine of the day was the four cylinder Ford. One racer chose to use a four cylinder Chevy engine. This was a fateful decision, because the exhaust was not on the right side of the engine for the crowd to see when the cars went by the grandstand. In those days, in that type of racing, it was generally assumed that the most free-flowing exhaust was no exhaust. A feature of every racing evening was having the Chevy guy drive his car around the track backwards so everyone could see the flames from his exhaust.

Most any performance parts shop will have a very large selection of exhaust components. Like many things in the performance market there are as many opinions about the "right" combination of performance as there are performance parts shop employees.

In most jurisdictions any exhaust headers that allow for the retention of all emission control devices are legal. However, in California and similar jurisdictions any modification to the exhaust from the catalytic converter forward must be California Air Resources Board approved.

## Headers

As has been previously explained, no exhaust system is not really the best exhaust system. There are many off-the-shelf exhaust systems that can greatly improve performance. At this writing, the California Air Resources Board approves some 49 exhaust related retrofit items, and there are many more approved for the other 49 states. As you can see, the modifications legal on the exhaust side of the engine are far more extensive than on the intake side. Here is a list of the legal components as per Code Section 27156:

| E.O. or Res. Number (Date) | Manufacturer "Product" (Model/Kit No.) | Vehicle applications |
|---|---|---|
| D-67 (7/28/76) | Crager Industries, Inc. "Hot Pipes" | **75-76** Catalyst equipped vehicles excluding those with backpressure modulated EGR valves |
| D-148 (10/16/84) | R.N.D. Enterprises "Heat Riser Adapter" | **74 and older** equipped with heated air and retrofitted with exhaust headers |
| D-149 (11/16/84) | Custom Speed and Marine "Preheat duct tube" | **74 and older** equipped with heated air and retrofitted with exhaust headers |
| D-161-24 (2/20/92) | Gale Banks Engineering "Exhaust Crossover Pipes" (P/N 52702-STD & P/N 52702-HO | **82-92** model-year V-8 powered Chevrolet Camaros and Pontiac Firebirds |
| D-161-27 (4/28/92) | Gale Banks Engineering "Powerpack System for 7.5L Ford or Oshkosh Chassis Motorhomes | **89-92** Motorhomes with GVW of 14,000 lbs. or greater powered by a Ford 7.5 liter EFI gasoline engine and utilizing the Ford or Oshkosh chassis |
| D-161-28 (4/28/92) | Gale Banks Engineering "Powerpack System for 7.4L P-30 Motorhomes | **90-92** model-year motorhomes with GVW of 14,000 lbs or greater powered by a General Motors 7.4L (454 CID) |
| D-164 (5/13/86) | Hooker Industries "Hooker Super Competition Header" P/N 2838 | **75-82** Chevrolet/GMC trucks and Blazer/Jimmy vehicles with an engine displacement between 305 and 400 CID, except catalyst equipped vehicles with feedback controls |
| D-165 (5/27/86) | Downey Off-Road Mfgr. "Exhaust Header" (No. 17410-R79S) | **79-80** Toyota 2 & 4-WD pick-up |
| D-166 (6/6/86) | Ermie Immerso Enterprises "Exhaust Header" (P/N 4644) | **79-80** Toyota 2-WD and 4-WD pick-up trucks with 20R engine |
| D-167 (7/3/86) | Hedman Header "Exhaust Header" (P/N 69097) | **78-82** Chevrolet 2-WD pick-up trucks equipped with 305 or 400 CID engine |
| D-167-1 (11/13/91) | Hedman Header "Exhaust Header") (P/N 89461 | **87-92** model Ford trucks powered by 7.5L EFI V-8 gasoline engine |

| E.O. or Res. Number (Date) | Manufacturer "Product" (Model/Kit No.) | Vehicle applications |
|---|---|---|
| D-167-2 (6/4/92) | Hedman Header "Exhaust Header" Model Nos. 79220, 79220-6, 79130, 79130-6 | **77-91** Chrysler Class C vans; 77-79 Chrysler 1/2-3/4 ton 2wheel drive trucks **88 and older** Chrysler Class A Motor Homes equipped with a catalytic converter and non-feedback controlled 361 to 440 engines |
| D-167-4 (6/2/92) | Hedman Header "Tubular Exhaust Manifold System" Model Nos. 68451, 68451-6, 69471, 69471-6, 68481, 68481-6, 69470, 69470-6, 69461, 69461-6 | **82-92** GM vehicles equipped with 305-454 CID fuel-injected engines |
| D-167-5 (6/2/92) | Hedman Header "Tubular Exhaust Manifold System" Model Nos. 88600, 88600-6, 89461, 89461-6 | **86-92** Ford Mustangs equipped with 5.0L engine; 87-92 Ford pick-up trucks equipped with 7.5L engine |
| D-167-6 (6/15/92) | Hedman Headers "Hedman Hedders" | **75-81** GM and Ford vehicle powered by 8 cylinder engines except those with feedback control |
| D-170 (10/29/86) | Mr. Gasket Company "Blackjack Exhaust Header" (P/N 3021-S) | **77-79** Chevrolet Camaro with a 305 or 350 CID engine |
| D-170-1 (10/29/86) | Mr. Gasket Company "Cyclone Exhaust Header" (P/N 10512-S) | **77-79** Chevrolet Camaro with a 305 or 350 CID engine |
| D-170-2 (10/29/86) | Mr. Gasket Company "Eagle Exhaust Header" (P/N 1021-S) | **77-79** Chevrolet Camaro with a 305 or 350 CID engine |
| D-180-14 (2/5/92) | The Turbo Shop "460 EFI Header System" | **87-92** Ford vehicles with 7.5L (460 CID) engines |
| D-180-15 (4/3/92) | The Turbo Shop "EFI Header System" | **73-87** GM Pickup, Suburban, Blazer, Jimmy with 283-454 CID 8 cyl. Engines (P/N 13-001 to 13-003, 12-001 to 12-003; 75-89 GM Class A Motorhome with 454 CID engine (P/N 12-001, 12-002); **80-92** Ford Pickups, Broncos, Vans, Mini Motorhomes, Class A Motorhomes with 302-460 CID 8 cylinder engines (P/N 11-001, 11-002, 6-012 to 6-014, 6-003) |
| D-187 (1/27/89) | Street Legal Performance Engineering, Inc. "Performance Package" | **85-88** GM Camaro and Firebird (F-Body) with 5.0L/5.7L tuned port injection engines |
| D-187-2 (1/27/89) | Street Legal Performance, Inc. "Tubular Exhaust Manifolds" (TRI-Y) | **85-88** GM Camaro and Firebird (F-Body) with 5.0L/5.7L tuned port injection engines |

| E.O. or Res. Number (Date) | Manufacturer "Product" (Model/Kit No.) | Vehicle applications |
|---|---|---|
| D-200 (5/15/90) | Doug Thorley Headers "Exhaust Header Part No. 300Y" | **74-80** GM trucks and Blazer/Jimmy's equipped with an engine displacement between 283 and 400 CID |
| D-200-1 (5/15/90) | Doug Thorley Headers "Exhaust Header Part No. 300Y CO" | **74-80** GM trucks and Blazer/Jimmy's equipped with an engine displacement between 283 and 400 CID |
| D-200-2 (12/6/90) | Doug Thorley Headers "Exhaust Header Model No. 248Y" | **80** model-year mini motor homes, trucks, vans, and Broncos equipped with a Ford 302-351 CID engine, excluding those with feedback control |
| D-200-3 (8/7/91) | Doug Thorley Headers "Exhaust Headers" Part Nos. 350, 375Y, and 308 | **75-79** Corvette equipped with a 283-400 CID engine; **75-77** Chevrolet Nova (excluding Malibu) equipped with a 283-400 CID engine; 75-79 Camaro Z-28, Chevelle, El Camino, Monte Carlo equipped with a 283 -400 CID engine; **78-79** Pontiac Grand Prix/Buick Regal, Olds Cutlass equipped with a 305 engine |
| D-200-4 (8/7/91) | Doug Thorley Headers "Exhaust Headers" Part Nos. 315Y | **75-81** GMC light duty trucks/medium duty vans and mini-motorhomes equipped with non-feedback 283-400 CID engines |
| D-200-5 (10/24/91) | Doug Thorley Headers "Exhaust Headers" Part Nos. 303Y-SO, 303Y-DAO8, 388Y-SO, 354Y-SO, 354Y-DAO, 393Y-SO, 399Y-SO | **87-92** GM vehicles powered by a closed loop 6.6-7.4 liter engine |
| D-200-6 (11/6/91) | Doug Thorley Headers "Exhaust Headers" Part Nos. 405Y, 405Y-S, 410Y, 410Y-S, 450Y, 450Y-S | **75-79** Datsun/Nissan pickups with 20LB or Z20E engine **75-77** Datsun/Nissan pickups with L18E engine **80-83** Datsun/Nissan pickups with Z20E or Z22E |
| D-200-7 (11/6/91) | Doug Thorley Headers "Exhaust Headers" Part Nos. 502Y, 502Y-S, 510, 513Y, 542Y, 542Y-S | **75-82** Toyota Celica with 20R or 22R engine **75-79** Toyota Landcruiser eith F (3.9L) or 2F (4.2L) engines **75-80** Toyota 2WD pickup with 20R or 22R engine **78-80** Toyota 4WD pickup with a 20R or 22R engine |
| D-200-8 (11/13/91) | Doug Thorley Headers "Exhaust Headers" Part Nos. 605Y, 605Y-S, 610, 610-S, 615Y, 615Y-S, 625, 625-S | **75-82** AMC Jeep CJ5, CJ6, CJ7, CJ8 with 304-401 CID engine **75-82** AMC Jeep CJ5, CJ6, CJ7, CJ8 |

| E.O. or Res. Number (Date) | Manufacturer "Product" (Model/Kit No.) | Vehicle applications |
|---|---|---|
| | | with 232-258 engine<br>**75-79** AMC Jeep pickup, Wagoneer, Cherokee with 304-401 CID engine<br>**80-82** AMC Jeep pickup, Wagoneer, Cherokee with 304-401 CID engine |
| D-200-9 (11/13/91) | Doug Thorley Headers "Exhaust Headers" Part Nos. 106Y, 106Y-S, 114Y, 114Y-S, 153, 153-S | **75-81** Plymouth/Dodge van with 273-360 CID engine<br>**80-81** Dodge Ramcharger, Dodge pick up, Plymouth Trail Duster with 273-360 CID engine<br>**75-76** Dodge Dart and Plymouth Valiant/Scamp with 273-360 CID engine<br>**76-79** Dodge Aspen/Diplomat, Plymouth Volare with 273-360 CID engine |
| D-200-11 (11/13/91) | Doug Thorley Headers "Exhaust Headers" Part Nos. 215, 225, 230, 265 | **77-79** Ford 4WD pickup with 351-400 CID engine<br>**80-81** Ford 2WD pickup with 351-400 CID engine<br>**80-81** Ford 2WD/4WD pickup and van with 351 or 400 CID engine<br>77-79 Ford 4WD pickup with 351 or 400 CID engine<br>**75-76** Mercury Cougar with a 351 or 400 CID engine<br>**75-78** Ford Torino/Fairlane or Mercury Montego/Cyclone equipped with a 351C or 400M engine |
| D-200-12 (11/13/91) | Doug Thorley Headers "Exhaust Headers" Part Nos. 203, 210, 211Y, 264 | **75-76** Ford 2WD pickup with 360 to 428 CID engine<br>**75-79** Ford 2WD pickup with 429-460 CID engine<br>**75-81** Ford 2WD van with 429-460 engine<br>**75-76** Ford 4WD pickup with 360-428 CID engine |
| D-200-13 (11/13/94) | Doug Thorley Headers "Exhaust Headers" Part Nos. 245Y, 245Y-S, 248Y, 263 | **78-81** Ford Courier pickup with 2.3L engine<br>**80-81** Ford 2WD/4WD Bronco, 2WD/4WD pickup and van equipped with 302W or 351W engine<br>**75-77** Ford 2WD/4WD Bronco equipped with 289 or 302W engine |
| D-215-2 (7/29/92) | Edelbrock Corporation "Tubular Exhaust System" | **82-92** GM passenger cars with 5.0L or 5.7L gasoline engine<br>**87-92** GMC LDT equipped with 4.3L V6, 5.0L V8, 5.7L V8, 7.4L V8 gasoline engines<br>**86-92** Ford passenger cars with 5.0L engines |

| E.O. or Res. Number (Date) | Manufacturer "Product" (Model/Kit No.) | Vehicle applications |
|---|---|---|
| D-216 (4/22/91) | J. Bittle American, Inc. "Short Header Model 1620" | **86-91** Ford Mustangs with 5.0L V8 EFI |
| D-216-1 (5/8/92) | J. Bittle American, Inc. "Short Header Model 1621" | **85** Ford Mustangs with 5.0L gasoline engines |
| D-216-2 (7/7/91) | J. Bittle American, Inc. "Short Header Model 1627 & 1628" | **85-91** Ford light duty trucks with 5.0L or 5.8L V-8 gasoline engine |
| D-216-3 (9/9/91) | J. Bittle American, Inc. "Short Header Model 1633" | **90-92** Ford or Mazda light duty trucks with 4.0L V6 gasoline engine |
| D-216-4 (1/16/92) | J. Bittle American, Inc. "Short Header Model 1620, 1624, 1627, 1628" | **85-92** Ford light duty trucks with 5.0L or 5.8L gasoline engine<br>**86-92** 5.0L Mustangs<br>**90-92** 5.0L Thunderbird (engine family MFM5.OV5FXFX)<br>**86-92** 5.0L Lincoln LSC with EEC-4 ECU and sequential EFI<br>**84-85** 5.0L LTD LX with EEC-4 ECU and central EFI<br>**79-84** 4.2L & 5.0L V8 Mustang with EEC-4 ECU<br>**80** 5.0L Crown Victorias with EEC-# ECU and Variable Veturi carb<br>**82-83** 5.0L Crown Victorias and Lincolns equipped with EEC-3 ECU |
| D-216-6 (9/24/92) | J. Bittle American, Inc. "Short Header Model 1629" | **88-92** Ford F-150 truck with 7.5 gasoline engine |
| D-226 (7/1/91) | J. Bittle American, Inc. "Turbolator" | **91** and older model year cars |
| D-237 (11/21/91) | S & S Headers, Inc. "Tubular Exhaust Headers" | **87-88** Volkswagen Rabbit and Scirocco with 1.6L engine |
| D-241 (12/5/91) | M.A.C. Products "Stubbie Header, Model No. 9028690 | **86-92** Ford Mustang with 5.0L V8 gasoline engine |
| D-241-1 (3/4/92) | M.A.C. Products "Stubbie Header and Shortie Header" | **86-92** Ford F-150, F-250 and Bronco with 5.0L or 5.8L V8 with EFI engine (Stubbie P/N 9358960)<br>**86-92** Ford Mustang with 5.0L V8 EFI engine (Shortie P/N 508692) |
| D-241-2 (7/22/91) | M.A.C. Products "Stubbie Header, Model No. 903091 | **90-92** T-Birds and Cougars with 5.0L V8 gasoline engine |
| D-249 (5/13/92) | BBK Performance Specialists "Equal Length Shorty Header" | **85-86** Mercury Capri<br>**85-92** Ford Mustang<br>**86-92** Lincoln Mark VII with 5.0 engine |

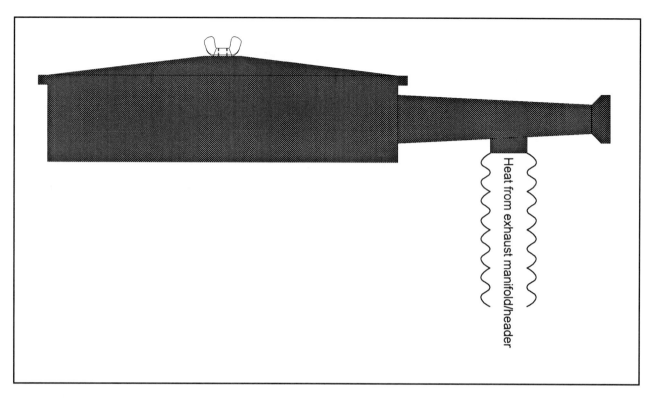

Heat from exhaust manifold/header

The hot air door is critical for cold weather operation. Cold weather or not, if the original configuration of the engine had a hot air door it is considered part of the emission control system and must be retained after mdifications are performed.

Left: On the visible side of this manifold, halfway down the manifold is a flat area provided for a choke heat stove. Under the heat stove there is a passageway for exhaust gases to pass through the manifold under the carburetor or throttle body injection unit. This warming of the manifold is to help keep the fuel in suspension during cold weather operation. This warming of the manifold will also decrease performance because it warms and expands the air mass destined for the combustion chambers.

## Preheating and heat riser

It may sound like a little thing, that is of course unless you live in the higher latitudes or the higher altitudes of North America, but warm air will keep the fuel atomized better than cold air. A cold intake manifold has a difficult time keeping the fuel droplets in suspension as they

Although it is less important to the fuel injection system than many believe, it is also more important to the fuel injection system than others believe. When planning your engine modifications be sure the exhaust gas oxygen sensor will remain in approximately its original position. Putting it too far away from the cylinder head exhaust ports will make it slow to warm up and therefore make it slow to enter the emission and fuel efficient "closed loop" mode. Locating it too close to the cylinder head exhaust ports will subject it to potentially damaging high heat.

Fuel injection systems offer a great boon to the performance oriented enthusiast. However, there are some areas where creativity is not permitted for legal or driveability reasons. The oxygen sensor is as important to the intake system of the modern fuel injection system as any of the other sensors. Fitted into the exhaust, it is used to help the computer control the air/fuel ratio.

travel through the manifold. A solution dreamed up a few decades ago was to warm the air before it enters the manifold, or in the central plenum area of the manifold. Intake preheating systems and intake manifold crossovers were the result.

It is a cold December morning. In the distance there is the sound of engine brakes on the big trucks on the interstate as they decelerate into Sheriff Billy Joe-Bob's Yankee trap. The cold air carries the sound well. You crank the engine on your 1970 Buick Skylark 350. With great hesitation it comes to life. The cold air struggles to carry the fuel through the intake. Within a few engine cycles the exhaust gases begin to heat the exhaust pipes. Surreptitiously, the air cleaner pre-heat door is drawing warm air off the exhaust manifold. The warm air is far more capable of keeping the fuel suspended as it is transported to the cylinders. Unfortunately, the warm air is less dense than the cold air. The less dense air entering the combustion chamber results in less power. A door in the snorkel of the air cleaner should change position as the underhood temperature rises. As insignificant a device as this may seem to the devout motorhead living in Yuma, Arizona, it is nonetheless required for the vehicle to be street legal if it had one when it left the factory. There are kits available to add this function to nearly any exhaust system.

Another covert device in maintaining good air/fuel mixing during warm-up is the exhaust cross-over of the intake manifold. This is a passageway that runs between the cylinder heads through the intake manifold. Exhaust gases pass through the cross-over to warm the air/fuel mixture. Since poor mixing of air and fuel as the mixture enters the combustion chamber can cause high hydrocarbon carbon monoxide emis-

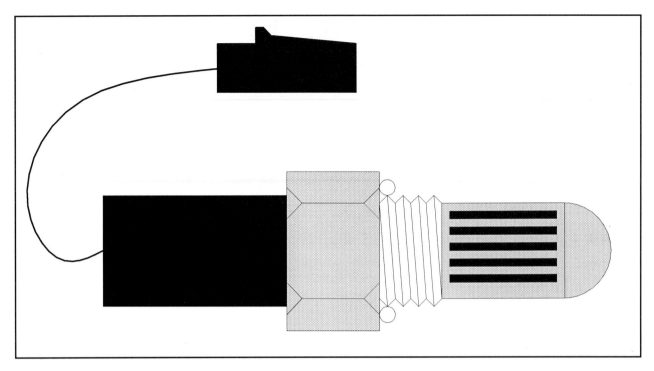

The oxygen sensor is used by the fuel injection computer or electronic carburetor computer to fine tune the air/fuel ratio. If the intake manifold allows any air to enter the engine without being measured by the carburetor venturi, the mass air flow sensor or the manifold pressure sensor the oxygen sensor is supposed to compensate. However, this assumes that the air leak affects the air/fuel ratio of all cylinders equally. This is never the case. Do not depend on the oxygen sensor to compensate for carelessness.

sions during warm-up, installing a manifold not equipped with a crossover on a street engine that is supposed to have one is illegal. Ironically, there are many technicians that claim some engines practically roll off the assembly line with the crossover restricted. Restricted crossovers account for many cold weather, cold running driveability problems.

## Location of the Lambda or "EGO" sensor

Now this is a bit of an art. The Exhaust Gas Oxygen sensor, also known as "oxygen sensor", "Lambda sensor", or "that little spark plug looking thing in the exhaust system" must be located close enough to the cylinder head to permit rapid warm-up after the engine is started. When the oxygen sensor is slow to warm up, emissions suffer, fuel economy suffers, and catalytic converter damage can occur. When the oxygen sensor is located too close to the cylinder head, it can overheat and be damaged.

Before purchasing a set of exhaust headers or other exhaust related component that may affect the position of the oxygen sensor relative to the head, be sure to compare the new $O_2$ sensor location to the old. Keep in mind that one of the benefits of some new exhaust header systems is their ability to retain heat. This will allow the oxygen sensor location to be further downstream. Generally, if the exhaust system component provides a place for the installation of the $O_2$ sensor, and if the component is CARB (California Air Resource Board) approved, then the sensor location is, with very little doubt, just fine.

## Pipes

Really, I suppose, the most important reason for the pipes is to save the driver from minor inconveniences such as a mild to serious case of death. Carbon mono-xide is a slow to virtually instant killer. I have read reports that claim the red, oxygen carrying, corpuscles of the blood have a 15 to 200 times greater affinity for CO than for $O_2$. Even the more conservative figure is frightening. In Kurt Vonnegut's novel "Slaughterhouse 5," the wife of the main character, Billy Pilgrim, dies of carbon monoxide poisoning. Billy had become the sole survivor of an airplane crash in the mountains. On her way to visit him in the hospital, the exhaust system is torn off her Cadillac. She dies of inhaling submicroscopic particles of an odorless, tasteless and colorless

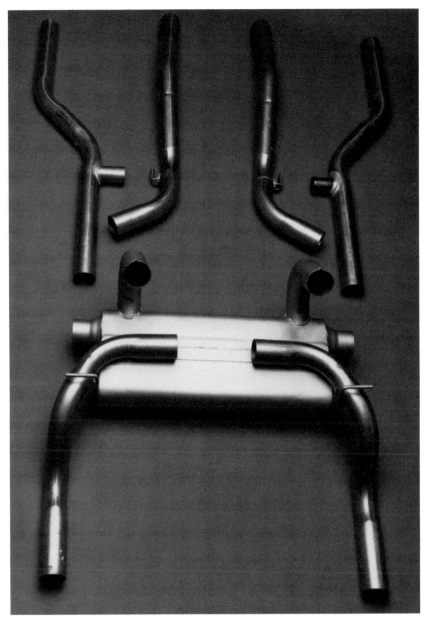

The pipes themselves can do little to increase performance. However, even in a race car the temptation to omit pipes can be a fatal one. If the exhaust gases are allowed to exit the exhaust system under the car poisonous carbon monoxide can enter the passenger compartment of the car, killing the passengers.

gas, while he survives a 20,000ft plummet into a snow-covered mountain. The irony of this tale illustrates well the danger of this gas.

Unfortunately, there are few who take the potential of CO poisoning seriously. All too many performance cars terminate their exhaust system under the car. I suppose there is a certain validity in people saying that the car will always be driven with the windows down, that the car will only be driven in the summer...that they are going on a diet tomorrow, that they will NOT vote for the incumbent next time. The car will almost assuredly be driven at some point with the windows up if the car is destined for street use. Do not kid yourself.

## The first Mustang pipes

If you remember my experience with the stove pipe and the Mustang referred to in a previous chapter, you might think that we only installed our sophisticated pipes to fool the tech inspectors. The truth is we were both concerned about the potential brain damage that would result from carbon monoxide poisoning. Yeah, right...I'm sure you believe that all 20-30 year old race drivers of the early seventies were worried about brain damage.

## Design
### Rear exiting

This is good, usually. The idea is to cause the exhaust gases to leave the rear of the vehicle and leave the driver and passengers safe from carbon monoxide and other noxious fumes. There are two dangers with this method, both related to making the pipes almost long enough, but not quite. If the pipes terminate below the trunk, then during an extended idle they can be drawn in to poison the occupants. In vehicles such as vans they can be drawn in as the vehicle moves down the road. The flat end of the van creates a low pressure area that can draw the fumes toward the doors. Make sure if the pipes run toward the rear of the vehicle that they terminate after the last body panel.

I suppose the topic of frictional back pressure versus performance should be addressed. First of all, if you are running a track car without windows, even a door slammer that will never see the street with your racing exhaust, feel free to terminate the exhaust anywhere you wish. This, of course, assumes you will never sit in long staging lines be-

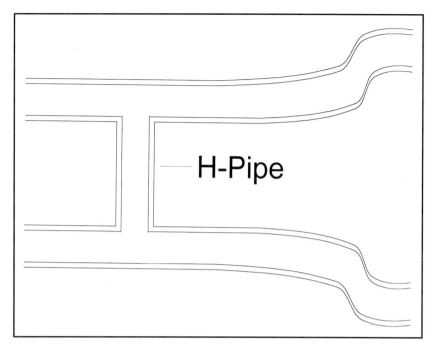

Most exhaust systems have an area where resonances and eddies build up in the exhaust gases. To reduce this build up on dual exhaust systems it helps to install an "H" pipe between the two sides of the exhaust.

hind half the drag cars of the western hemisphere, that long lines of those inferior beasts we call the competition will pull aside when they see you approach. I do not mean to be a curmudgeon about this, but there is considerable evidence that even relatively small quantities of CO can destroy brain cells and over many years do brain damage. There are enough people who think that those of us who prefer to spend money on fire breathing power than on Microsoft stock already suffer from too few brain cells. But do not take my word for that, just ask your wife, or your girlfriend soon after she becomes your wife. She will be glad to tell you.

The disadvantage of rear exiting pipes is the long run the exhaust gases have to make through them. Each inch of travel adds frictional resistance and therefore back pressure.

## Side exiting

These are just cool. Back in the days when Parnelli Jones was just finishing his Pony Car career and before he became better known for Firestone stores in the southwest, I used to race in competition with a fellow named Alf. Alf owned a BMW 2002 with an exhaust system that exited on the right. The unwritten rule was to never let Alf pass on your left, unless you had plenty of cotton in your ears.

Everyone knows that flaming side pipes were the hit of the early to mid-seventies. That is, of course, until girlfriends who had fathers rich enough to support the race car started burning holes in their nylons getting in and out of the car.

Seriously, the greatest advantage of the side exiting pipe is the relatively short run the exhaust gases have to make before leaving the exhaust system. This reduces the frictional resistance of the exhaust system and improves performance. If the pipes exit behind the rear post of the rear-most doors on the car, you are reasonably well protected from carbon monoxide

poisoning. Again, many with performance as their prime consideration will terminate the exhaust as soon as possible after the headers. This may put them at just the right place to pollute the interior of the vehicle.

## Materials

There are no hard and fast rules for the type of materials to be used. In reality the stove pipe, not counting its potential for leaks and CO poisoning, was a good choice. Light weight is important for a performance car. Every pound added to the weight of the car decreases performance.

It sometimes seems odd to me that in this world of complex electronic systems, instant communications, and high technology that we would even think about discussing technological advances in a metal tube. Nevertheless, I am about to do so. Years ago there were two jobs I dreaded getting when I reported to the service dispatcher. One was a tune-up on a big engine in a small Ford; the other was to change any exhaust component on any car. By the time the typical consumer got around to replacing their exhaust parts, they were rusted to the point of disintegration. As soon as these parts were touched they would collapse into an avalanche of rust flakes. Today this problem is rare.

There are several reasons that rusted-out pipes are rarer today than in the past. One of the main reasons relates to a favorable by-product of an event of the seventies that is often viewed as the worst performance event in the automotive industry of the past 2000 years, unleaded gas! Tetraethyl lead formed an acid in the exhaust system that destroyed the system from the inside out. Also, metallurgy has changed to the extent that today the exhaust system may last as long as the practical life to the car. Today there are several metals commonly used in exhaust systems.

## Low carbon steel

Low carbon steel contains less than 0.08 percent carbon by weight. This results in a smooth, homogeneous blend which stands up fairly well to corrosion and physical stress. This used to be one of the most commonly used materials in standard exhaust systems and inexpensive "performance" systems. Low carbon steel was the direct cause of the aforementioned avalanche of rust flakes. While it served rather well for short periods of time, the use of these steels brought about the advent of national chains of muffler shops. When the industry moved to other metals it caused these national muffler chains to branch out into brakes or tune-ups to survive.

## Aluminum coated steel

Coating low-carbon steel with an aluminum silicon alloy protects the steel from corrosion and increases the life expectancy of the exhaust system.

## Stainless steel

Stainless steel is an expensive way to reduce the effects of corrosion. Virtually impervious to corrosion, "stainless" systems can often outlive the vehicle. The drawback (and of course all things automotive are a compromise), is that most stainless steels are very brittle. Two types of stainless steel—Type 304 and Type 409—offer good corrosion resistance and reasonably good resistance to cracking and damage from vibration often associated with the brittleness of stainless steel.

## Galvanized steel

I have a personal problem with this one. When I was a kid I used to go camping with my parents. When I was about 7 years old we bought a galvanized bucket as a camp utility vessel. I have real difficulty in using anything on my car that even smacks of a "bucket". Everytime I hear the term *galvanized* I think of that bucket. Nevertheless, the galvanizing process provides reasonably good corrosion protection.

## The "H" pipe
### Purpose of the "H" Pipe

In the intake section of this book there was a great deal of time spent discussing the concept of pressure waves and resonances. Most exhaust systems have an area where resonances and eddies build up in the exhaust gases. To reduce this build up on dual exhaust systems, it helps to install an "H" pipe between the two sides of the exhaust. However installing the "H" pipe in the wrong place does more harm than not installing one at all. Bad guesses do not count.

### Locating the "H" Pipe

To determine where an "H" pipe is needed on your custom dual pipe exhaust system, paint the area between the catalytic converters and the mufflers with black lacquer. Run the engine at 3200rpm for several minutes. Now inspect the painted area. Where the lacquer has begun to burn, or has burned the worst, indicates the place where the "H" pipe needs to be installed. Install the pipe between the indicated hot-spots on the two side of the exhaust.

## Mufflers

Looking back again to the sixties, we saw a fascination among street enthusiasts with bigger pipes and "freer" exhaust flow. Today's stock exhaust systems are a far cry from the stock systems of the sixties. In spite of this there is still room for improvement.

Muffler systems and their technology have come a long way since the muscle car days of the sixties. Today's high performance mufflers exceed the flow potential of even open headers.

There are two things that travel down the piping from the exhaust manifold—exhaust gases

A new generation of performance mufflers offers quiet performance far superior to the performance of the older street racer systems. These new mufflers make full use of newer understanding and theories of gas flow and acoustics. In the Flowmaster brand muffler exhaust gases flow along using the same principles as the waves have on the surfers at Wieamea Bay on the north shore of Oahu.

Flowmaster makes mufflers suitable for just about any application.

and sonic vibrations, or waves. The movement of the waves through the exhaust system tends to pull the exhaust gases along in much the same way that ocean waves pull a surfer to shore. The effect of the exhaust

gases being pulled through the exhaust system helps to scavenge the cylinder, improving the breathing of the engine.

Back in the sixties, several companies marketed the "Turbo" muffler, developed by Chevrolet

for the Corvair Turbo. It consisted of a hollow tube with fiberglass pressed against the sides of the tube to deaden sound. The problem with this is that as the sound frequencies enter the muffler they are killed by the fiberglass packing, negating the "surfer" effect.

Today's hi-tech performance mufflers are able to reduce sound without eliminating the "surfer" effect. Imagine for a moment that you are setting up a stereo in your living room. The only place you can find to put one of the speakers is in the center of the north wall. The only place that you can find to put the other speaker is directly opposite the first, on the south wall. The two speakers are facing each other squarely. The only place you can find to put your chair is exactly half way between the two speakers. When the speakers are producing exactly the same sound, the waves being emitted from the two speakers will collide and cancel one another, creating a dead zone. Modern high performance mufflers take advantage of this phenomenon. As the exhaust gases enter the muffler, they are divided and sent in two different directions, only to be brought back together as they pass though the muffler. When they are brought back together, the identical frequencies collide and cancel each other, like the speakers described earlier. The end result is less sound without a loss of the "surfer" action.

Mufflers such as those described here are currently being used on everything from road racers to sprint cars.

## Muffler brands

Mufflers are of little importance to the EPA. I did not say of no importance, just of little importance. Of all the areas of intake and exhaust modifications, the area where you can have the most fun and the most options is

The intent of the Flowmaster design is to maximize the "surfer" analogy mentioned earlier. The chambers create resonances of "anti-pressure" (you Trekkers should know what that is) that are phased to the backpressure pulses of the exhaust gases.

The result is that the anti-pressure nuetralizes the backpressure while the chamber muffles the sound. The result is an exhaust system with almost no back pressure and an acceptable noise level.

128

Many "performance mufflers are simply high flow variations of stock designs. For most street performance applications they provide acceptable performance levels.

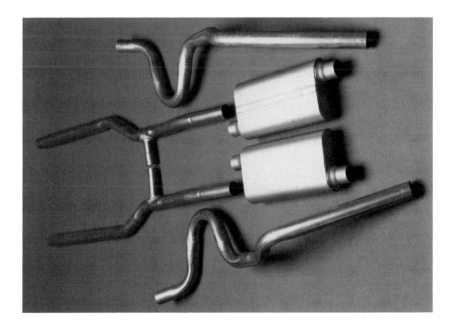

For the perfomance minded individual with plenty of money and a fair amount of skill there are complete kits available. These kits feature all the pipes and mufflers necessary for installation. In some cases these kits require welding. Check with your local muffler shop about installation if you, like your author, are not skilled with the blue-tip glue.

the muffler. Because of this the last several years have seen an explosion of muffler brands and designs.

### Flowmaster

Flowmaster, Inc., is located in Santa Rosa, California. The Flowmaster muffler consists of a series of chambers that create a "wave" action which actually pulls the exhaust gases along. Their literature claims that, when properly tuned with the correct length pipes, the system will actually create a vacuum where the exhaust gases enter the exhaust system.

The intent of the Flowmaster design is to maximize the "surfer" analogy mentioned earlier. The chambers create resonances of "anti-pressure" (you Trekkers should know what that is) that are phased to the back pressure pulses of the exhaust gases. The result is that the anti-pressure neutralizes the back pressure while the chamber muffle the sound. The result is an exhaust system with almost no back pressure and an acceptable noise level.

In addition to mufflers, Flowmaster offers a line of performance exhaust system kits precisely designed to improve the power and fuel economy of almost any performance car.

### Dynomax

Dynomax is a product line of Walker Manufacturing, a Division of Tenneco. Walker is a brand name muffler you might have had installed at Ward's, Sears, or just about any auto repair shop. Their approach to mufflers and exhaust is more traditional than that of Flowmaster.

### Thrush

A name that reminds me of sitting in high school assembly, as a junior, listening to the student body president orate "ad nauseam" about something or other is Thrush. This popular manufactur-

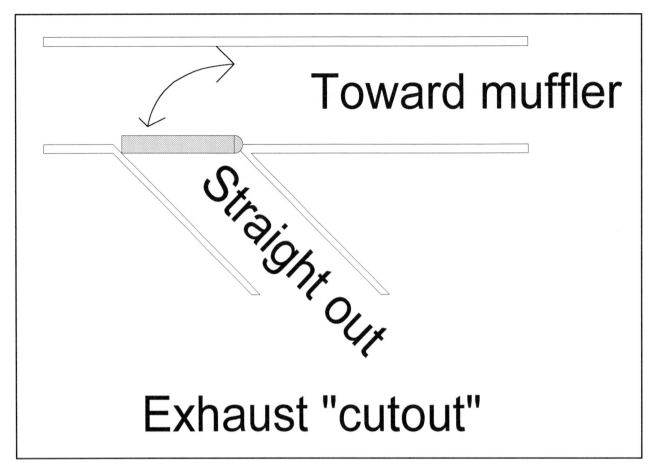

**Toward muffler**

*Straight out*

**Exhaust "cutout"**

Exhaust muffler bypasses are right out of the movie American Graffiti. Although they may make the engine sound powerful, in reality they can actually inhibit rather than improve exhaust gas flow.

er of performance exhaust parts has for years offered street performance exhaust systems. Their repertoire includes glass-packs and a variety of exhaust assembly parts. Today, among the many exhaust parts they offer, they are one of the few manufacturers of high flow catalytic converters.

*NOTE:* Some things *never* change. That student body president is now my Congressman.

### Catalytic converters

A good stock catalytic converter used on a mildly modified engine is quite capable of flowing freely. Remember, however, that the limit to the effectiveness of any airflow related modifications on a street car is the amount of gas that can flow through the catalytic converter. As was previously stated the stock catalytic converter can probably handle virtually any streetable modifications. Nonetheless the converter remains the single exhaust component that allows the least number of legal options. All other components can be extensively modified, the converter cannot. What performance modifications increase airflow? Well, in keeping with the well-established theory that power comes from airflow, just about every modification.

• Camshaft
• Intake manifold
• Carburetor
• Fuel injection throttle body
• High-ratio rockers

• Headers
• High flow mufflers
• Turbochargers
• Superchargers
• High speed pistons and connecting rods allow for higher engine speeds and therefore greater air and exhaust flow.

The catalytic converter is the limiting factor because it is the one device in the exhaust that cannot be altered or removed. Thrush makes a performance converter that they claim has lower back pressure (greater flow rate) than stock converters. While I have very little doubt that their claims are accurate, I would recommend the following (this suggestion assumes you are either good friends with the local dealer or have so much money that...):

Take the "performance" converter and several stock converters to your local owner of a cylinder head flow bench. Slip him an extra $20 to put together a set-up to check converter flow rates, and test these several converters for flow. This is analogous to matching connecting rod and piston weights. Today many people just buy "balanced" rods and pistons, in the "good old days" we would buy 48 rods and pistons for a V-8 engine and try to find the best match of parts. Today no one builds a true "racing" converter. Since no two parts are ever exactly the same, individual units need to be tested for best potential performance.

## Exhaust muffler bypasses (cut-outs)

When I was a little younger, back before you could not trust anyone over 30, there were several things every "performance" car had to have. These items were: a dog with a bobbing head on the rear window package tray, lights in the fender wells, furry dice hanging from the rear view mirror, and muffler cutouts. The cutouts were located in the down pipes between the exhaust manifold and the front muffler. When performance was needed, a cable would be pulled or a lever thrown, allowing the screaming power sound of the engine exhaust to bypass the muffler and go straight to the atmosphere. The main problem with this is that not only would the sound go to the air under the car, but so would the carbon monoxide.

A further problem is that the cut-outs themselves create a tremendous amount of turbulence and restriction. If someone with a gray D-A haircut suggests cutouts for track to street flexibility, remind him that the Dodgers are no longer in Brooklyn.

## Some other performance exhaust manufacturers

- Borja
- CVX
- Cyclone
- Hooker
- Hedman
- Blackjack

# Chapter 12
## Intake related emission controls

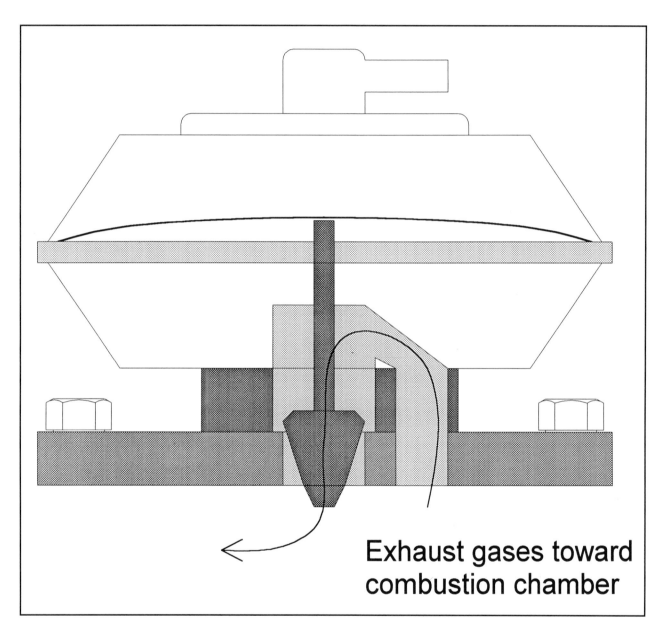

**Exhaust gases toward combustion chamber**

The EGR valve meters a small amount of exhaust gases back into the intake system. Once in the intake system they find their way to the combustion chamber. In the combustion chamber they absorb heat from the combustion process and reduce the emissions of oxides of nitrogen.

Left: EGRs valve are generally opened by vacuum. It is strictly and federally illegal to disable the operation of the EGR valve.

## Exhaust gas recirculation (EGR)

The master bard of the sixties said, "There's a fog upon L.A." It might have been more accurate for him to say that there was a *smog* upon L.A. Among the principal components of this *photochemical smog* are oxides of nitrogen, often referred to as "NOx". The EGR valve is used to reduce the production of oxides of nitrogen.

The amount of NOx increases as the load on the engine increases because as the load on the engine increases, the combustion temperature also increases. When the temperature of combustion increases above 2500 degrees F, oxygen from the atmosphere begins to combine with nitrogen from the atmosphere, the result is a plethora of gases known collectively as "oxides of nitrogen." Some of these gases are harmless, one of them you may have enjoyed at the dentist's office. Some of them, $NO_2$ for example, is another story entirely. A nasty photochemical reddish-brown haze results when some oxides of nitrogen are dumped into the atmosphere. Additionally, oxides of nitrogen are linked to some forms of acid rain.

As the throttle is opened and engine rpm rises above idle, either vacuum applied to a diaphragm, or a solenoid lifts the pintle of the EGR valve. This allows exhaust gases into the combustion chamber. Approximately 7 percent of exhaust gases in the combustion chamber volume will lower the burn temperature by about 500 degrees F. This lower temperature reduces the production of NOx.

When replacing intake manifolds for street performance, there is always the temptation to install a manifold that does not use an EGR valve. In the first place, if your car or engine came from the

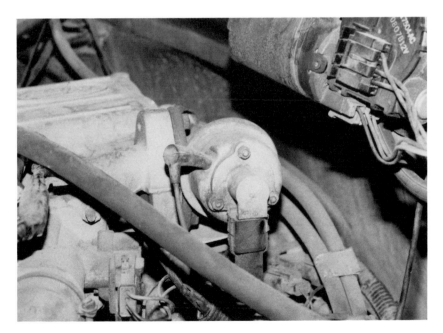

This Ford EGR valve uses a potentiometer located on the top of the EGR valve to report the position of the EGR valve. If the valve opens too much too soon it can cause hesitation and even stalling. This feedback sensor improves the computer's control of the EGR valve.

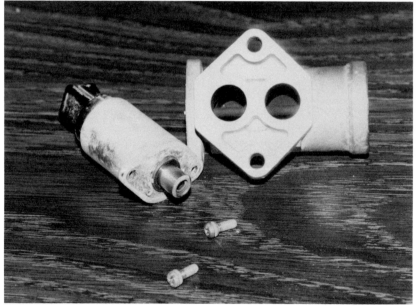

Above: Some later model Ford applications use a differential pressure sensor to detect the position of the EGR valve. This PFE (Pressure Feedback EGR) sensor compares the pressure in the exhaust to the pressure in the intake manifold to detect how much the EGR valve has been opened by the computer.

Left: Fuel injected applications use the process of "bleeding" air from upstream of the throttle plates to downstream of the throttle plates to control idle speed. When selecting a replacement manifold or throttle asembly for these applications be sure that there is proper provision for the idle air bypass control valve.

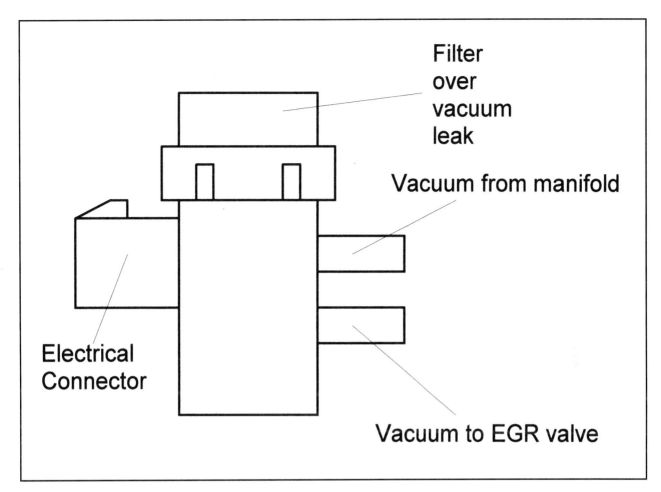

Filter over vacuum leak

Vacuum from manifold

Electrical Connector

Vacuum to EGR valve

Above and next page: On many applications the EGR position is controlled by the computer. Vacuum is bled off on many of these when the computer wishes the valve to be closed. A soleniod operated control valve is used by the computer to control whether or not the EGR valve is opened. Do not bypass this solenoid when installing a replacement manifold.

factory equipped with an EGR valve, it is a violation of Federal law to operate that car or engine on the street without an EGR valve. Additionally, the EGR valve helps to control combustion temperatures. With the EGR removed or disabled, combustion temperatures can rise to the point where engine damage can occur.

## "Programmed" vacuum leaks

I can hear it now. "Watson, you must be nuts; why would there be a 'programmed' vacuum leak?" On some applications, such as most Ford engines, the EGR receives vacuum all the time. A normally open solenoid operated valve bleeds the vacuum to the atmosphere until the computer wants the EGR valve to open. At that point the solenoid operated valve closes and the EGR valve opens.

"Doesn't that cause a problem?" With all that vacuum leaking out all over the place, isn't there damage to the environment?" Actually vacuum leaks do not exist. They are, in fact, leaks of air into the intake system. These air leaks lean the air/fuel ratio. When the intake manifold is replaced with a street-type manifold, great care must be taken to ensure that all of these "programmed" vacuum leaks are retained. If a street/performance manifold is used these vacuum/air leaks can adversely affect performance. It may be necessary to redesign the EGR control system. Whatever you do to the EGR system should be okayed by an emission testing referee before the modification is made. A word to the wise: in California and some other states such modifications are forbidden.

# Chapter 13
# Exhaust-Related Emission Controls

## Lambda or "EGO" sensing

One of the most critical emission control components in the exhaust system is the oxygen sensor. This sensor is sometimes referred to as the EGO or *exhaust gas oxygen* sensor. Almost all of the cars made anywhere in the world to be sold in North America use a "platinum" oxygen sensor. It is essentially the same sensor whether it is in a Ford Festiva or a Lamborghini Countach. There is another sensor that has seen some duty on North American delivery Jeep and Eagle products—the "titania" oxygen sensor.

## Operation
### Platinum

The oxygen sensor, sometimes called a Lambda or EGO sensor, might be described as a chemical generator. Once operational temperature is reached, the sensor will begin to respond to changes in the oxygen content of the exhaust.

When the engine is running rich, there is a low oxygen content in the exhaust and a high voltage is produced; when it is running lean, there is a high percentage of oxygen, and a low voltage is generated. At the point of perfect combustion, known as the stoichiometric point, the oxygen sensor produces 450 millivolts.

When the oxygen sensor voltage is low, indicating a lean condition, the computer will respond by enriching the mixture. When the oxygen sensor voltage is high the computer will respond by leaning out the mixture. In this manner the computer adjusts for minor errors and variations from the rest of the input sensors and controls the air fuel ratio at 14.7:1.

The thimble shaped oxygen sensor consists of a zirconium oxide ceramic which becomes permeable by oxygen ions at

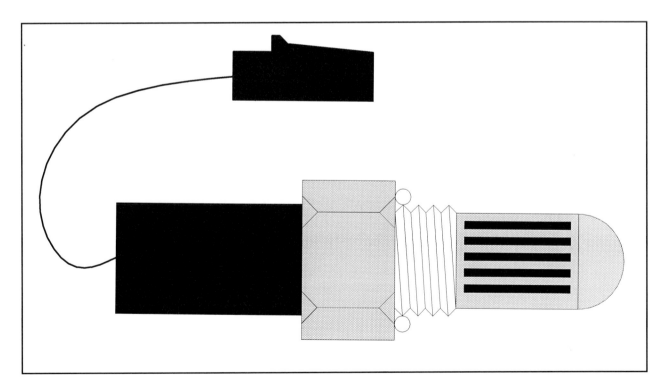

The oxygen sensor detects the amount of oxygen in the exhaust. The computer uses this information to adjust the amount of fuel being injected into the engine.

The oxygen sensor screws into the exhaust system. The location of the oxygen sensor is critical. In the exhaust section of this book we will look at the location and relocating of the oxygen sensor.

Many peopke like to use silicone when the intake manifold is installed. This helps to reduce the risk of intake manifold leaks and the subsequent air fuel ratio problems. Although I feel that these sealants are often used as a substitute for careful repair work, conservative use does have its place. Above is an oxygen sensor safe silicone sealer. The phrase "Low Volatile" confirms that this silicone sealer will not damage the oxygen sensor.

300 degree Celsius. One part of the ceramic is located in the exhaust stream while the other is exposed to ambient oxygen. The surface of the ceramic is covered with a thin, gas-permeable layer of platinum. When the percentage of oxygen contacting the two ends of the ceramic is equal, there is a balance of oxygen ions and no voltage is generated. When there is an imbalance oxygen ions are attracted from the surplus side and a voltage is generated. The oxygen sensor output voltage varies from about 100 to 900 millivolts during normal engine operation.

Many applications have a very high impedance circuit which will replace a missing oxygen sensor signal with a default voltage of 450 millivolts. This voltage can be detected with a high impedance voltmeter whenever the oxygen sensor is cold or disconnected.

## Common Defects

The oxygen sensor will very seldom develop a defect. It is, however, very susceptible to contamination. Common contaminates are:
• Tetra-ethyl lead
• RTV silicone
• Soot

As noted earlier, the placement of the oxygen sensor with respect to the exhaust ports of the cylinder head is critical. If replacing the exhaust manifold with headers causes the oxygen sensor to be located too far downstream, it will take too long to warm up after a cold start and it will cool down when exhaust volumes are low. These problems can result in incorrect air/fuel mixture, emission problems, fouled spark plugs and driveability problems. Many of the later model oxygen sensors are equipped with a heater. The heater makes exact placement of the sensor a little less critical.

This silicone sealer might damage the oxygen sensor and should not be used to seal the intake manifold or any other engine components.

If the oxygen sensor is located too close to the exhaust ports of the cylinder head it can overheat—the exhaust gases could literally burn the tip off the sensor.

138

In short, try to locate the oxygen sensor as close to its original position with respect to the cylinder head as possible.

### Titania

In North America the titanium oxygen sensor is used exclusively by Jeep/Eagle. Unlike the platinum oxygen sensor, the titanium oxygen sensor is not a voltage generator, but rather a variable resistance that responds to changes in exhaust oxygen content.

The sensor is fed a five volt reference through a resistor inside the computer. As the oxygen content of the exhaust increases, the resistance of the sensor increases, so the voltage between the computer and the oxygen sensor rises. When the oxygen content of the exhaust decreases, the voltage between the computer and the oxygen sensor decreases. The result is that a rich exhaust produces a low voltage and a lean exhaust produces high voltage.

Like the platinum oxygen sensor, the location of the titanium oxygen sensor is critical. This sensor does not operate efficiently until its temperature is over 1400 degrees Fahrenheit. Although equipped with a heater, the placement of the sensor relative to the cylinder head is even more critical than it is with the platinum oxygen sensor.

### After burning systems—Thermal
### Air pumps

The air pump has three purposes. The first is to help heat up the oxygen sensor and the catalytic converter when the engine is warming up. The second is to add oxygen to the hot exhaust gases as they leave the cylinder head which helps to convert carbon monoxide and hydrocarbons in the gases into relatively harmless carbon dioxide and water. The third job is to add oxygen to the mixture in the catalytic converter to improve its efficiency.

Air is pumped into the exhaust manifold while the engine is cold. Since a rich mixture is present in the combustion cham-

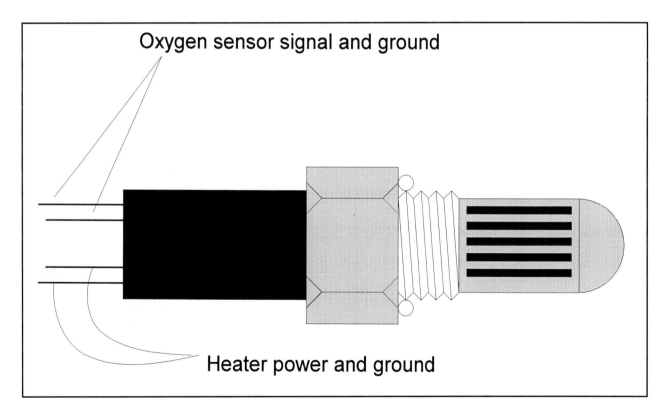

Oxygen sensor signal and ground

Heater power and ground

In North America the titanium oxygen sensor is used exclusively by Jeep/Eagle. Unlike the platinum oxygen sensor, the titanium oxygen sensor is not a voltage generator. This oxygen sensor is a variable resistance similar to the coolant sensor's thermistor. Instead of responding to temperature, however, the titanium oxygen sensor responds to changes in exhaust oxygen content. The sensor is fed a five volt reference through a resistor inside the computer. As the oxygen content of the exhaust increases the resistance of the sensor increases. Therefore, the voltage between the computer and the oxygen sensor rises.

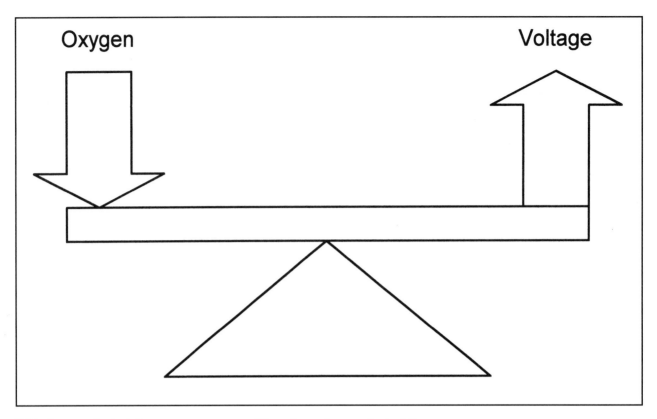

Oxygen

Voltage

With the standard platinum oxygen sensor as the oxygen content of the exhaust drops during rich running conditions the voltage output of the oxygen sensor rises.

ber at this time, the resulting exhaust gases will be laden with CO and HC. The air pump injects air into the exhaust manifold. When the oxygen in the air meets with the CO and HC their temperature increases dramatically and "afterburning" takes place. The afterburn consumes much of the residual CO and HC.

As a side benefit from this afterburning a great deal of heat is generated. The heat assists in bringing the catalytic converter and the oxygen sensor up to their proper operating temperature.

Before the ECM goes into its *closed loop* mode it is necessary for the air being pumped by the air pump to be diverted either to the atmosphere or downstream of the oxygen sensor. The downstream air is often pumped into the center of the catalytic converter. This helps to improve the

efficiency of the second stage, or oxidizing stage, of the catalytic converter.

It is essential that the relatively common practice of disconnecting or eliminating the air pump not happen. First and most obviously, it is illegal. The presence of air, both during the warm-up process and afterwards, is essential to permit the oxygen sensor and the catalytic converter to operate properly. If the oxygen sensor does not operate properly, driveablity problems can occur with electronically fuel injected cars and those equipped with an electronic carburetor.

**Upstream/downstream valves**

It has already been pointed out that the air pump is fairly essential to the proper operation of the emission control devices. I know what you are thinking at

this point, "Gee, if I was really interested in emissions rather than performance I probably would not have "Hurst" permanently embedded in the palm of my hand." And I agree. However, proper operation of this equipment on cars where it is required allows for a whole new generation of street rods. Priced a '66 Mustang or '69 Chevelle lately? There is a lot of potential in a '78 Olds Cutlass (and, no, it does not really need to be called an Olds Gutless). To make such a car legal for street performance, the emission control devices must be left in place and be operable.

This brings me back to the air pump switching valves. These valves control the operation of the air pump, diverting air into the upper part of the exhaust near the head when the engine is

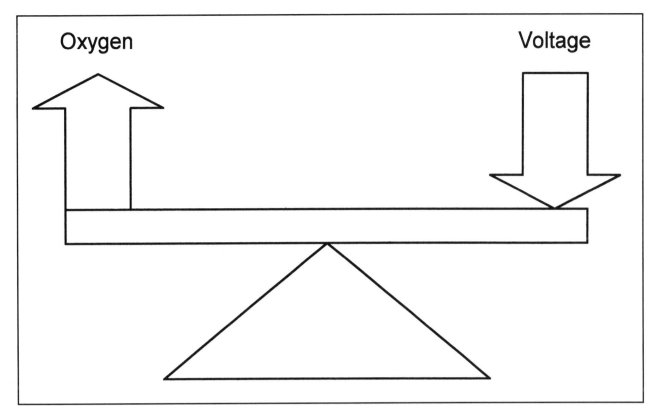

Oxygen

Voltage

As the oxygen content of the exhaust increases during lean running conditions the voltage output of the standard platinum oxygen sensor falls.

cold to preheat the oxygen sensor and the catalytic converter and directing it down to the converter when the engine is at operating temperature. But most important of all to you and your wallet, if they are malfunctioning or connected wrong, they may allow air to pump upstream of the converter during deceleration, or into the converter during deceleration, and on a carbureted car that can cause an explosion in the exhaust that could leave hundreds of dollars of exhaust parts as scrap iron in the middle of the road.

These switching valves are connected to either thermal vacuum switches on the intake manifold or to computer controlled vacuum solenoids. Proper connection and routing must be assured in order to prevent expensive explosions and emission test failures.

### Check valves

Hoses run from the air pump to the steel tubes connected to the intake manifold. These hoses are attached to the steel tubes through a check valve. When these check valves become damaged or ruptured, hot exhaust gases can make their way to the air pump switching valve and the air pump itself, causing severe heat damage. The easiest way to check the valve is to drive the car around the block several times then grab each of the hoses with your hand. If you regret touching the hoses due to pain from the heat, the check valve is fine. If you *really* regret touching the hose, the check valve needs to be replaced.

### Catalytic converters
### Oxidation catalyst

In 1975 I was working in an auto repair facility in Arlington, Texas. A lady came in with a brand new car she had just purchased a few days earlier. Her complaint was that the passenger side floorboard of the car was getting extremely hot and she was afraid to drive the car back to the dealer. We checked out the problem. There was a funny front muffler under the car that seemed to be getting extremely hot. We told her that we did not think that it was supposed to do that and sent her to the dealer. Of course this funny muffler was the catalytic converter.

When the catalytic converter was introduced in the 1975 model year it was designed to reduce carbon monoxide and hydrocarbon emissions. It accomplished this by providing an environment where extra oxygen could be added to these chemicals to yield carbon dioxide and

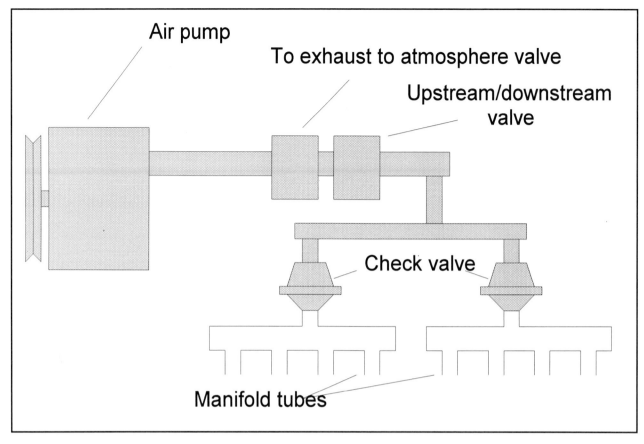

Air pump

To exhaust to atmosphere valve

Upstream/downstream valve

Check valve

Manifold tubes

Air pumps are one of the oldest emission control devices. Typically they rob less than one horsepower from the engine. Although they have a rather high failure rate and are often deliberately disabled, this is illegal.

water. This "oxidizing" converter consisted of platinum coating a ceramic substrate. These early converters came in two categories—monolithic and beaded. The monolithic converters resembled a honeycomb, while the beaded resembled, well, beads.

From the outset, these converters were accused of causing everything from poor performance to high blood pressure. The truth is that a typical catalytic converter will have many times the cross section area of the pipe leading into it. As a result, any increase in back pressure was caused by friction, not restriction. What problems there were with performance and catalytic converters were usually brought on by inexperienced or poorly informed people trying to increase power from the engine.

In order for the oxidizing section of the catalytic converter to work efficiently and not suffer damage, the air/fuel ratio must be 14.7:1 or leaner. Unfortunately for many of the performance minded, there is the misconception that more fuel means more power. Enthusiasts would replace carburetors, replace jets, or drill out jets, all with the goal of increasing power. Any of these operations could enrichen the mixture beyond 14.7:1. The result of sending the exhaust gases from a rich mixture through the catalytic converter would be to increase the operating temperature of the catalytic converter. When the converter overheats, the substrate begins to melt and the melted substrate restricts the exhaust.

A properly modified street performance application should be fully compatible with the catalytic converter. Among many there is still the mistaken view that air fuel ratios have gotten leaner in the past two decades. This is both true and untrue. I have a book that was published in 1947 that states the proper air fuel ratio was 10,000 parts of air to one part of fuel by volume. Today this ratio is expressed by weight, yet 10,000 parts of air to one part of fuel *is* 14.7 parts of air to one part of fuel by weight.

What we cannot do is what was common practice in the sixties—cover up a poorly thought out design by enrichening the air/fuel ratio much beyond 14.7:1. Bolting on a "fat" carbu-

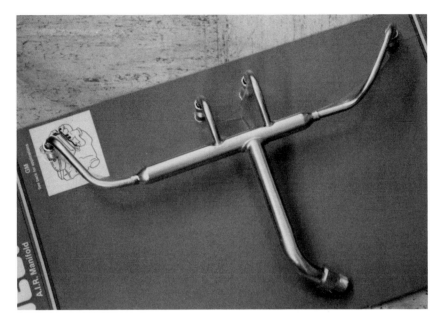

When you add performance exhaust parts you may need to replace parts in the air pump system. Do not short cut legality for the sake of performance. This A.I.R. manifold will not only replace one of the most chronically rusted items but will also make the end product of the modification look nice.

retor will no longer work. If the carburetor is going to put in more fuel, then the intake system, the valve train and cam shaft, the cylinder head, the pistons, the swept volume of the cylinders and the exhaust system must allow for enough airflow to permit proper combustion. If there is proper combustion the catalytic converter, not to mention your friendly neighborhood emission tester, will operate efficiently and effectively with no damage.

There is still the temptation among some to remove the cat-alytic converter. This is a definite violation of Federal law and, frankly, the length of pipe you replace it with may have more restriction and back pressure than the converter.

## Reduction catalyst

In the late seventies and the early eighties a second section was added to the original catalytic converter. Located up stream of the oxidizing catalyst on modern automobiles is the reducing catalyst. The job of the reducing catalyst is to break down oxides of nitrogen NOx into their base components of oxygen and nitrogen. The reducing catalyst works best when the air fuel ratio is richer than 14.7:1. As far as the performance enthusiast is concerned it is unlikely that he/she would deliberately make the air/fuel ratio leaner. Just slightly to the lean side of the perfect air/fuel ratio performance begins to suffer. The performance minded and the reducing catalyst are therefore totally compatible.

## 3-way catalyst and performance

There is little doubt or room for conflict in the idea that a catalytic converter is the limiting factor in the power potential from the engine. However, if the car is going to be used on the street in the United States or its territories, the catalytic converter must be left in place. For the street performance enthusiast it should be comforting to know that most legal modifications will not increase the airflow capacity of the engine enough for an undamaged converter to be of concern. If your emissions jurisdiction permits major modifications to the engine while requiring the converter to remain in place, ask before the modifications are done to the engine if it would be legal to install a larger capacity converter. Also let me know where in North America that jurisdiction is; I may want to move there.

# Chapter 14
## ——How a Turbocharger Works——

**Theory**

The theory of the turbocharger is simply this: *Cram in more air and you will get more power.* Earlier in this book a great deal of time was taken to explain that the goal of the air induction system, the cylinder head design and the exhaust system was to fill the cylinder with a mass of air at atmospheric pressure equal to 100 percent of the volume of the cylinder with the piston at bottom dead center. When this is accomplished it is said that the engine is operating at 100 percent of volumetric efficiency. There are many things that prevent this. It was also discussed that a great deal of energy is lost to the heat of the ex-

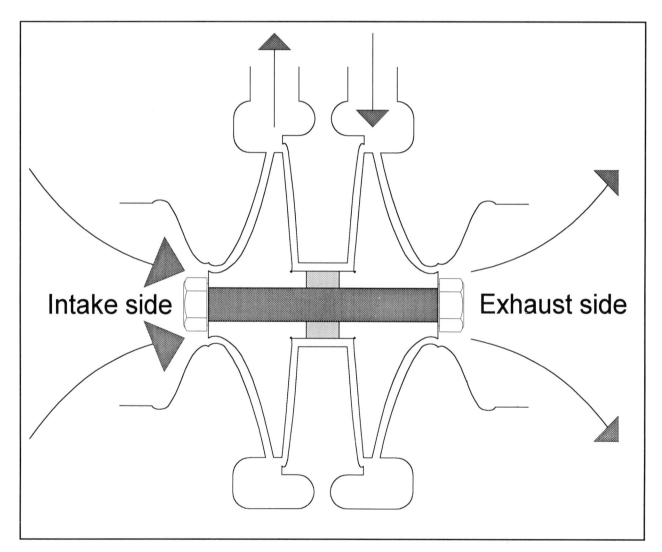

Intake side            Exhaust side

A turbocharger is an exhaust driven supercharger. The heat and velocity of the exhaust gases are converted into rotary motion to drive a compressor. A turbocharger uses the wasted heat energy of the exhaust gases to power a pump which forces air into the cylinder to achieve 100 percent volumetric efficiency or greater as often as possible.

haust gases. A turbocharger uses the wasted heat energy of the exhaust gases to power a pump which forces air into the cylinder to achieve 100 percent volumetric efficiency, or greater, as often as possible. The concept is pure in its motives—using wasted power to create power.

## Turbine

Several years ago I was asked to do a class on turbochargers for a group of mechanics in Vancouver, British Columbia. Mechanics in Canada, as a group, are considerably different in their attitude from most mechanics in the United States. U.S. mechanics taking a class tend to want to know the minimum that will be necessary to do their job. Canadian mechanics tend to want to know things about the subject which really have nothing to do with their job. Knowing this I proceeded to the university library in Anchorage. Since I was teaching a class in Anchorage at the time, it was more convenient than going to the library in my home town of Fort Worth. I expected to be asked by these Canadian mechanics how the simple flow of exhaust gases past an impeller can create rotary speed well in excess of 60,000rpm. After much digging through dusty volumes I found what I wanted. It is important to note that people in Anchorage are in their right minds. This is attested to by the fact that these volumes were dusty.

Imagine that the turbine impeller of the turbocharger (the exhaust drive side) is a pinwheel. The mere flow of the exhaust gases past this pinwheel is not enough to account for the terrific speeds attained by the tur-

Right: Some waste gates also use manifold pressure (vacuum) to assist in accurate control of the turbo boost.

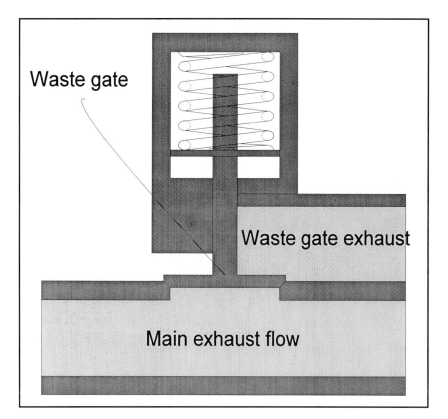

A pressure control valve located in the exhaust system will open when the pressure in the exhaust exceeds a predetermined point. The spring tension can be changed to alter the amount of boost.

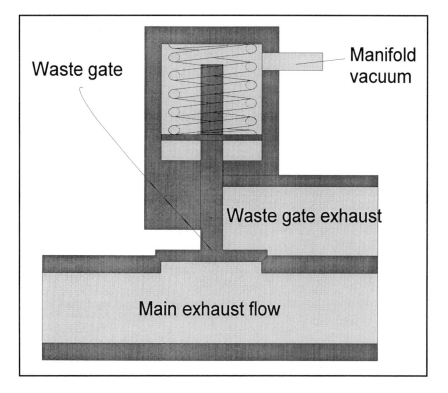

bocharger. Can you imagine a pinwheel reaching 60,000rpm even in a hurricane? The fact is that the exhaust gases contain a lot of energy in the form of heat. As the exhaust gases pass across the impeller, the heat energy is converted to rotary motion.

## Compressor

In the wide world of compressors there are many types. There is the axial, the piston, the positive displacement and the centrifugal. The centrifugal compressor is reserved for two divergent areas, refrigeration compressors of the size that is used in shopping centers and indoor sports arenas, and turbochargers. Great rotational velocity is required to get pressure from one of these compressors.

Much earlier in this book we talked about a 100mi tall column of air pressing down on the intake valves of the engine. When the valve opens the air pushes its way into the combustion chamber.

Now imagine an enormous thunderstorm, the bottom of which is just above the top of the intake valve. In a thunderstorm warm air rises thousands of feet above the ground, where it is cooled. The cool air then comes crashing to the ground at great velocity. Our thunderstorm is 100mi high. The "cool" air falls with great velocity against a closed intake valve. The velocity of the entire air column being the same a pressure is created against the intake valve as the molecules from a layer immediately above the intake valve to 100mi above the intake valve push their way toward the valve.

The result of this commotion is a high pressure against the valve. When the valve finally opens the air molecules rush in filling the combustion chamber to a pressure higher than atmospheric. Decrease the velocity of the air column and you decrease the commotion and the rush to get into the combustion chamber.

When the high velocity column of air meets with an obstruction such as a closed intake valve or the top of a piston (when the intake valve is open) the velocity is converted to pressure.

Other types of compressors create pressures by trapping the air, squashing it, then releasing it in its squashed form. The centrifugal compressor works only by accelerating the air. Decreasing the speed of the compressor decreases the velocity of the air and therefore the potential pressure of the air in the combustion chamber. In fact, as the speed of the turbocharger increases, the potential pressure increases by a square of that increase. In other words, if you double the speed of the turbocharger compressor, the potential pressure is quadrupled. Quadruple the speed of the turbocharger compressor and the potential pressure will be 16 times greater. All of this means that the speed of the turbocharger is critical. If it spins too slowly, potential air pressure will remain quite low. If it spins too fast, the intake manifold will overpressurize, the intake manifold temperatures will go above acceptable levels, and combustion temperature will increase exponentially until metal parts of the engine begin to melt.

## Control

There are several ways the output boost of the turbocharger is controlled. The simplest is to use a turbocharger suited to the engine such that boost pressure can never exceed specified boost limits. For instance, many diesel engine applications run no control on the turbocharger boost while the turbocharger is in operation. When a huge turbine is used in a huge diameter exhaust pipe and installed on a small engine, the comparatively small exhaust gas volume will prohibit high turbine speeds. When the turbine speed is low, boost is low. Now increase the size of the en-

gine and decrease the size of the turbine. The increased exhaust gas volume will cause the speed of the turbine to increase dramatically. When turbine speed increases, the compressor speed will, of necessity, increase as well, and boost goes up. If the relationships between engine size, maximum engine rpm, exhaust gas volume, and turbine size are properly proportioned, then exhaust gas output at maximum engine speed will not permit turbine speed to produce overboost. This is the simplest way to control boost, but this method never really obtains the maximum potential from the turbocharger.

A second, and very common method, is the waste gate. There are several configurations for a waste gate. The simplest is the poppet valve configuration. In this method a valve in the intake system opens a valve in the exhaust system whenever intake manifold pressures reach a predetermined point. If this valve is set for 15psi, then when boost pressures in the intake manifold exceed 15psi, the high pressure in the intake manifold will open the waste gate valve. This valve, however, does not vent intake gases to the atmosphere. Instead it diverts exhaust gases around the turbocharger turbine. The compressor speed drops and boost is limited. Often the relief pressure of this valve is controlled by the tension of a spring and is therefore easily adjusted.

My first experience with turbochargers was with the 1978 SAAB 99 Turbos. I remember that all of the authorized SAAB technicians in the dealership were issued a lead seal tool. This tool mashed and imprinted a piece of lead to ensure that the customer did not tamper with the wastegate adjustments. This is because it is safe to say that the life expectancy of the engine is inversely and exponentially proportional to the amount of boost. Although I find turbochargers to be a fascinating and exciting performance tool, they may also be very dangerous to the engine.

For factory turbocharger applications, electronic control of the boost is becoming evermore popular. In this system intake manifold pressure is monitored by a pressure sensor. The monitoring device is much like a manifold absolute pressure sensor, however it detects atmospheric pressure as only the mid-range of pressures it can read. When the intake manifold pressure, or boost, exceeds the limit prescribed by the programming of the computer, a solenoid operated valve will open to bypass the exhaust gases.

Additionally, an intake manifold air temperature sensor (also called a manifold charge temperature sensor) may be used. Since the intake manifold pressure and temperature are directly related, and since high intake manifold temperature translate directly into high combustion temperatures, the computer may be programmed to bypass exhaust gases whenever the intake temperature exceeds a predetermined point.

## Lubrication

There is an old story that, like many old stories, may have little foundation in fact, but does illustrate the importance of lubrication in turbochargers. It seems that an organization had a pair of Kenworth tractors with turbocharged diesel engines in San Diego, California. Another branch of the organization had a need for these tractors in Marysville, California. The tractors were loaded on a 40ft flatbed trailer, fifth wheels forward, and hauled to Marysville. Since the noses of the Kenworths were facing to the rear, as the airflow hit the exhaust stacks the rain caps were flipped open. Air flowed through the exhaust, through the engines, and out the intake. During the entire trip, the

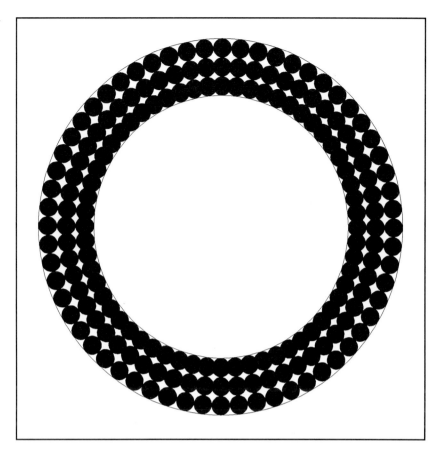

The shaft to the turbocharger rides on a film of oil. After driving the vehicle at high speeds or any time after driving under boost it is essential to allow the turbocharger to spool down (or slow down) before shutting the engine off. If the engine is shut off without spooling down the turbocharger severe damage can occur to the turbocharger shaft.

turbochargers were spinning without lubrication and therefore destroyed. Now you may have some of the same technical questions I have concerning open valves, coincidence, etcetera, that I have, but it is a good illustrative story.

There are many cases where damage is done to a turbocharger by "riding the engine hard and putting it away sweaty." Imagine traveling down the road at 64.99-mph. The engine rpm is about 2300, the turbo rpm is about 60,000. As you pull off the freeway, you shut off the engine. The turbocharger is now spinning at 59,000rpm with no lubrication. Turbo failure is inevitable.

A ball bearing will not work effectively at 60,000rpm. Most turbocharger bearings are therefore semi-floating or full floating oil film bearing. In the semi-floating design, the bearing is locked into place in the housing of the turbocharger, while the shaft that connects the turbine to the compressor floats freely in the bearing on a film of oil. If you are of the philosophy that the engine oil should be changed once a year whether you really need to or not, then forget turbochargers as a way of getting power out of your engine. While it is not really necessary to use a special "Turbo" engine oil it is advisable to choose one of the name brand, high quality, engine oils.

The oil filter is also important. Since most turbocharger installa-

| E.O. or Res. Number (Date) | Manufacturer "Product" (Model/Kit No.) | Vehicle Applications |
|---|---|---|
| D-89 (4/24/79) | Roto-Master, Inc. "Roto-master Turbocharger Kit" | 75-76 Mercedes 240D |
| D-90 (9/20/79) | RV Turbo, Inc. "RV Turbo Model No. 440-1" (Rajay turbo) | 79 and older heavy duty vehicles with Chrysler 440 CID engines |
| D-97 (5/5/80) | BAE "Dodge 440 Motorhome System" (No. 9-0000) | 79 and older heavy duty vehicles with Chrysler 440 CID engines |
| D-97-1 (10/3/80) | BAE "BAE Turbocharger Kit" (No. 28-0000C) | 80 VW Rabbit, Scirocco, and Jetta with manual transmission |
| D-97-7 (10/17/81) | BAE "Turbocharger Kit" (No. 3-0000W1) | 80-81 BMW 633i and 733i |
| D-97-16 (1/24/83) 83 BMW 533i | BAE "Turbocharger Kit" (No. 3-0012) | 82-83 BMW 633I and 733I |
| D-97-17 (2/7/83) | BAE "Turbocharger Kit" (No. 2-000-1) | 80-83 BMW 320I |
| D-97-18 (5/20/83) | BAE "Turbocharger Kit" (No. 32-0000-1) | 81-83 VW Rabbit, Dasher, Jetta, and Pick up with 97 CID diesel |
| D-97-19 (5/29/83) | BAE "Turbocharger Kit" (No. 28-0000-3) | 81-83 VW Rabbit, Dasher, Jetta, Pickup and Audi 4000 with a 105 CID engine |
| D-97-20 (7/29/83) | BAE "Turbocharger Kit" (No. 60-0002/4 HD) | 83 GMC HD vehicle powered by a 6.2 liter diesel |
| D-97-21 (8/9/83) HD Isuzu diesel | BAE "Turbocharger Kit" (No. T04B M2) | 81-83 Airstream motorhome powered by a |
| D-99 (2/29/80) | Turbonetics, Inc. "Turboflo 360" | 79 and older vehicles with Chrysler HD 360 CID engine |
| D-99-1 (11/19/86) | Turbonetics, Inc. "Turbotronic Turbocharger System" (Model No. 454 TCI-HD) | 87 and older Chevy/GMC 454 CID gaso line engine |
| D-112-1 (2/5/82) | Turbo International "Turbocharger Kit" (No. 301-E) | 82 and older Chevrolet vehicle with 305 and 350 CID engine equipped with an au tomatic transmission |
| D-112-2 (7/28/83) | Turbo International "Turbocharger Kit" (No. 4500) | 77-83 GM medium-duty and heavy-duty vehicles powered by a 454 CID engine |
| D-114-4 (5/23/85) | Martin Turbo Engr., Inc. "Turbocharger Kit" (No. 301 E10) | 85 and older GM 305 82 and older GM 350 |
| D-135 (8/11/83) | Diesel Research and Developement Corp. "Turbocharger Kit" (No. 482) | 83 and older Mercedes Benz 240D |
| D-140-14 (12/20/85) | Spearco Performance Products, Inc. "Turbocharger Kit" | 82 Supra (#9898) 83 Supra (#9899) |

| E.O. or Res. Number (Date) | Manufacturer "Product" (Model/Kit No.) | Vehicle Applications |
|---|---|---|
| | | 83 Cressida (#9900) |
| | | 82-84 Supra (#9909) |
| | | 83-84 Cressida (#9910) |
| | | 85 Supra & Cressida (#9909-A) |
| | | 86 Supra & Cressida (#9909-B) |
| D-140-21 (9/18/87) | Spearco Performance Products, Inc. "Turbocharger Kit" | 87 and older Toyota with a 2.4L fuel injected engine |
| D-142-1 (12/19/83) | Cummins Engine Co., Inc. "Turbocharger" (P/N 3029513, 4 &5) | 75-79 Cummins Heavy-Duty 092, 092A, 093E |
| D-155 (4/5/85) | Legend Turbo, Inc. "Turbocharger System" (Model VW-34) | 84-85 VW Jetta, Rabbit, Scirocco powered by a 1.8L fuel injected engine |
| D-161-4 (12/1/86) | Gale Banks Engineering "Turbocharger Kit" (Kit No. 6.9FR) | 83-87 Ford heavy-duty vehicles powered by a 6.9 International Harvester diesel engine |
| D-161-14 (9/26/90) | Gale Banks Engineering "Turbocharger Kit" (Kit No. | 83-87 Ford heavy-duty vehicles powered by a 6.9 International Harvester diesel engine |
| D-161-25 (5/14/92) | Gale Banks Engineering "Turbocharger Kit" (Kit No.) | 88-92 Ford heavy-duty vehicles powered by a 7.3 Navistar Harvester diesel engine |

tions share oil and oil filtration with the engine, it is necessary to use a high quality oil filter. Check with the supplier or manufacturer to ensure that their filter can stop all particles larger than 30 microns. Also remember that many engine oil filtration systems feature a bypass function. When the oil filter becomes restricted a bypass valve opens to allow unfiltered oil to pass through the engine. This prevents oil starvation as a result of poor maintenance. While this in the short term will *usually* do minimal damage to the engine, it can be disastrous to the turbocharger.

### Effect on emissions

As far as hydrocarbons and carbon monoxide are concerned, the turbocharger will have little effect. However, anytime you cram air into the combustion chamber to a level greater than 100 percent volumetric efficiency, the temperatures of the gases under compression will rise. Any time the temperature of the compressed gases in the combustion chamber rise, the combustion temperatures will also rise. When the temperature of the combustion exceeds 2500 degrees F, oxides of nitrogen will form. This makes many bolt-on turbo applications illegal. Below is a list of the legal and California Air Resources Board (CARB) approved applications.

It should be noted that the above information came directly from the California Air Resources Board. While it is the most current available at the time of publication, many of the above manufacturers may have subsequently had additional products approved. Also keep in mind that some of the products listed above are not turbocharger installation kits but rather turbocharger modification kits.

### Modern turbocharger design

One of the limitations of a centrifugal compressor turbo-charger is overcoming the inertia of the turbine and compressor. Exhaust gas flow changes anytime there is a change in demand placed on the engine by the driver. Increased demand is accompanied by increased exhaust gas volume. If the turbine and compressor had no inertia, the speed of the compressor, and therefore the velocity of the air moving toward the combustion chamber, would change immediately. Unfortunately these components do have inertia. As a result, there will always be a lag between change in horsepower demand and boost.

### Materials

Materials used in turbochargers must be of a type that will not be damaged or distorted by high temperatures or high rotational speeds. This has traditionally meant the use of heavy cast metals. Today ceramics are being put to work in turbochargers. These afford excellent durability with a minimum of inertia.

# Chapter 15
# —— Choosing the Right Turbocharger ——

In the early eighties I was employed by a small import auto repair shop in Kirkland, Washington. We had a young customer who wanted to turbocharge his Datsun 510. He had obtained a turbocharger from a friend who had taken the turbocharger off of a Pinto 2300 engine. The engines were similar in size, but this was no guarantee that it would work well. In this chapter we will discuss how to know what is the right turbocharger for a given engine and given use. Before selecting a turbocharger, a few basic questions have to answered. First, what is the use of the vehicle? Is the vehicle to be used to haul a salesman over a 5,000mi route, or to run 8 seconds at a time down a quarter mile, or over a bog? Second, what kind of maintenance will be performed on this vehicle?

## Engine application and selecting maximum boost pressure

For the purpose of discussion, let us say that we wish to add a turbocharger to a 1975 AMC Gremlin with a 258 inline 6 cylinder engine. Cars like this excite me more than Corvettes and Mustangs. After all, if at the Saturday night drags, a Mustang beats a Corvette, people will talk about it the next day, but if both are beaten by a Gremlin it is a major topic of discussion until at least the next Saturday night. We want to obtain maximum power/boost at 5000rpm. We wish that boost to be 20lb. The ambient temperature is 70 degrees F, and the ambient air pressure is 29.92in of mercury.

## Pressure ratio

To calculate the pressure ratio we must first know estimated airflow of the engine.

$$\frac{Engine\ CID}{1728} = Cubic\ feet\ displacement$$

$$CFD \times \frac{Max\ RPM}{2} = ideal\ cfm$$

$$ideal\ cfm \times 0.8 = estimated\ actual\ cfm$$

$$\frac{258}{1728} = 0.1493\ Cubic\ feet\ displacement$$

$$0.1493 \times \frac{5000}{2} = 373.25\ cfm$$

$$373.25 \times 0.8 = 298.6$$

$$Pressure\ ratio = \frac{Atmospheric\ Pressure\ Absolute + Boost}{Inlet\ Pressure\ Absolute}$$

$$Pressure\ ratio = \frac{29.92 + (20 \times 2.03)}{29.92}$$

(Note: the above 2.03 converts PSI into inches of mercury.)

Pressure ratio = 2.36

## What is pressure ratio

The pressure ratio is the pressure in the intake manifold under boost compared to atmospheric pressure. In the above example, the atmospheric air pressure is about 30in of mercury. After boost, the intake manifold pressure is about 40.6in of mercury above atmospheric. This means that the total pressure in the manifold is 70.6in of mercury. This pressure is 2.36 times greater than atmospheric.

## Estimating the temperature rise

When the air is forced, or compressed, into the intake manifold, its temperature rises. As the temperature rises, the air will expand. As a result, the air in the manifold ends up being pressurized, but expanded air. The amount the temperature rises can be accurately estimated.

Pressure/Temperature change factor = Pressure ratio $^{0.283}$ -1

Ideal temperature change = Pressure/Temperature change factor (Ambient temp + 460)

| Vehicle use | Torque/ Speed Range | Power Burst Duration | Suggested maximum boost |
|---|---|---|---|
| Street car | As wide as possible | 10 seconds maximum | 10 PSI |
| Road racer | As wide as possible | Some short, some long | 20 PSI |
| Drag racer | Medium to high | 10 seconds maximum | 20-30 PSI |
| Oval track racer running methanol | Medium to high | Almost continuous | 45 PSI |

Pressure / Temperature change factor = $2.36^{0.283} - 1 = 0.27507$

Ideal temperature change = 0.27507 (70 + 460) = 145.79

The 460 in the above formula converts the ambient temperature in degrees Fahrenheit to degrees F absolute (also known as Rankine). Notice that the above formula calculates the ideal temperature change. This formula assumes that no heat will be transferred from the turbine to the compressor side of the turbocharger. This, of course, is never so. The amount of transferred heat varies from one turbocharger to another. The formulas below will estimate the actual temperature change and the estimated actual temperature of the air in the intake manifold. Compressor efficiency is a measure of the amount of useful work available from the compressor, in the form of increased air pressure, compared to the amount of heat put into it. The difference is lost as heat. In other words, compressor efficiency is the amount of unused heat energy transferred from the turbine side of the turbocharger to the compressor side. Compressor efficiency is given as a percentage. A typical turbocharger would have an efficiency of between 65 percent and 85 percent. If you do not know the efficiency of the turbocharger you are working with, use the conservative figure of 65 percent.

Actual temperature change =

$$\frac{\text{Ideal temperature change}}{\text{Turbocharger efficiency}}$$

Intake manifold temperature =

Actual temperature change +

Ambient temperature

Actual temperature change $= \dfrac{145.79}{0.65}$

$= 224.29$

Intake manifold temperature = 224.29 + 70 = 294.29

## Density ratio

As the air in the intake manifold is heated through pressure increase, and with heat trans-ferred from the turbocharger turbine, the air expands. However this "expanded" air is trapped within the confines of a manifold with fixed dimensions. The expansion of the air causes the air in the fixed dimensions of this manifold to be less dense. The less dense air will have less power creating oxygen in it than if the air had not been made less dense through heating. The following calculation expresses the density change or *density ratio.*

Density ratio = $\dfrac{\text{Inlet temperature} + 460}{\text{Output temperature} + 460}$

$\qquad$ x $\dfrac{\text{Outlet pressure}}{\text{Inlet pressure}}$

Density ratio = $\dfrac{70 + 460}{294.29 + 460}$ x $\dfrac{40.6 + 29.92}{29.92}$

This means that the actual estimated cfm at 20lb of boost will be 1.66 times greater than it would be without the turbo. Since the estimated cfm was 298.6, the cfm under boost should be about 496. This 66 percent increase in cfm will also translate into an approximate expected increase in horsepower of 66 percent.

## Reading compressor maps

When the turbocharger manufacturers design and begin to market a new product, they will have a wide variety of data to distribute with the new design. Among this data should be found a "Compressor Map." This data sheet plots the compressor pressure ratio on the vertical axis, and the boosted cfm on the horizontal axis. Running from the lower left corner of the chart toward the upper right is a curving diagonal line known as the *surge line.* If plotting the pressure ratio against the maximum cfm intersects at a point to the left of the surge line, the cfm demand of the engine will exceed the turbocharger's ability to keep up. When well to the right of the line, the turbocharger will do a good job of feeding the engine compressed air.

## Multiple installation

I love talking with people who "know a lot about race cars." I remember going to a drag strip near Dallas, Texas, in the mid-seventies and being told by a spectator that a certain car was so fast because it had 4 camshafts. Now I know that a lot of racing engines, even in those days, had multiple camshafts, and I know that multiple camshaft, multiple valve configurations can improve intake and exhaust gas flow. I even know that there are adaptor kits available to convert stock-block engines into these multi-cam fire-breathers, but this was a bracket racer—a basically stock 396. However, ever since I have tried to apply the theory that the more you have of something the faster the car will go...more cams, more power tools, more turbochargers.

There are situations when a multiple turbo configuration may be useful. The most common use of multiple turbochargers is in a V-engine application. Because most V-engines are relatively large (2.5+ liters), the turbocharger required to adequately boost airflow would also have to be very large. A large turbocharger means a large rotating mass in the form of the turbine and compressor. Large rotating masses mean lag. Treating the V-engine as two smaller inline engines and using a separate and smaller turbocharger for each engine bank will reduce turbo lag. An added benefit will be reduced plumbing requirements.

## Reducing turbo lag

Although it was by no means the first turbocharged car I had ever driven, one of my most memorable "first-time" experiences with a turbocharged application was the first Datsun 280ZX Turbo I ever drove. At the time I owned an auto repair shop and had several "curb-side car dealers" as customers. One of them brought me this ZX concerned about a hesitation. After much troubleshooting and hand-wringing I learned that it was normal to put your foot to the floor and allow the traffic light to go through a complete cycle before the car would begin to accelerate. This is, of course, an exaggeration, but wholly illustrative of the sensation.

The most effective way to reduce turbo-lag is to reduce the rotating mass. Lighter materials are playing an important role in turbocharger development today. If your "go-racing budget" does not look like the national debt, custom made turbochargers using exotic materials are probably out of the question. Consider twin turbos.

## The personal computer and the turbocharger

Below is a BASIC program for calculating cfm airflow with the turbocharger at boost. If you have a personal computer, this program will run in all recent forms of BASIC in which I have tried it. You will definitely find this easier than the "by-hand" calculations which were discussed earlier.

```
CLS
INPUT " What is the cubic inch displacement of the engine? ", CI
INPUT " Engine speed you curious about air flow?               ", rpm
INPUT " Is this a two stroke or a 4 stroke engine?             ", Cycles
INPUT " At what boost PSI do you want to know air flow?        ", Boost
INPUT " What is the ambient temperature?                       ", Temp
INPUT " Current barometric pressure in inches of mercury? ", Baro
PRINT " What is the compressor efficiency?"
INPUT " Use 0.65 if you do not know.                           ", CEF
            CF = CI / 1728
            IDcfm = CF * (rpm / (Cycles / 2))
            Acfm = IDcfm * .8
            PR = ((Boost * 2.03) + Baro) / Baro
            Y = (PR ^ .283)—1
            TI = Y * (Temp + 460)
            TA = TI / CEF
            IT = TA + Temp
            DR = ((Temp + 460) / (IT + 460)) *
            (((Boost * 2.03) + Baro) / Baro)
            BCFM = ACFM * DR
PRINT
PRINT
PRINT , "The unboosted theoretical CFM is:"; IDCFM
PRINT , "The unboosted probable CFM is:"; ACFM
PRINT , "The pressure ratio is:"; PR
PRINT , "The temperature changector is:"; Y
PRINT , "The ideal temperature increase is:"; TI
PRINT , "The actual temperature increase is:"; TA
PRINT , "The intake temperature under boost is:"; IT
PRINT , "The density ratio is:"; DR
PRINT , "The boosted CFM is:"; BCFM
```

# Chapter 16
# —— A Supercharger is not a blower ——

As a youth in the sixties, trapped as an American in England, trapped by the fact that the only haircut the barbers on the base where my father was stationed knew how to give was white sidewalls, I went into the Star & Stripes and bought a magazine called *Cartoons*. I was hooked. Drag cars, slicks, 409's and blowers. Now, for years I thought that a blower was used to increase intake manifold pressure to get more horsepower. Then, one day, I was talking to a Detroit diesel mechanic when he pointed out that the job of the blower was to charge the cylinders on a 2 stroke Detroit engine. However, this oil burner technician did not realize that in the fifties motorheads adapted these 2 stroke

The "blown motor" was the ultimate fantasy of me and many of my cronies in high school in England. Many of these kids would have been more at home on the Ventura Highway than Carnaby Street.

Paxton makes a wide variety of superchargers for a wide variety of applications. Many of these are compact enough to fit covertly under a stock hood.

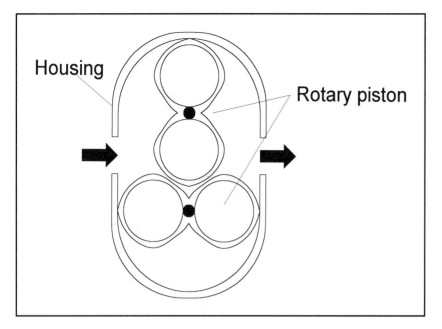

The Roots-type supercharger uses two interweaved symmetrical rotary pistons to force air into the intake system. The rotary pistons are synchronized by an external gear set. These synchronizing gears are then driven by the engine crankshaft by means of either a belt or, on rare occasions a gearset. The "Jimmy blower" type supercharger is the classic example of a Roots type.

blowers into superchargers for drag cars. Since those days, this crude adaptation has evolved into a high-tech industry.

The primary difference between the turbocharger and the supercharger is that where the turbocharger is driven by the exhaust gases, the supercharger is driven by the engine itself. Turbochargers feature a greater increase in power as the speed of the engine increases. This biases the power increase toward the higher rpm's. The engine driven supercharger gives a proportional increase in power throughout the rpm curve.

Until recently superchargers have been reserved for the drag strip or for the real motorhead. Today auto manufacturers are installing superchargers on luxury cars.

## Types of superchargers
### Roots
The Roots-type supercharger uses two interweaved symmetrical rotors to force air into the intake system. The rotors are synchronized by an external gear set. These synchronizing gears are driven by the engine crankshaft by means of either a belt or, on rare occasions, a gear set. The "Jimmy blower" type supercharger is the classic example of a Roots type. This supercharger is by far the most common.

### Sliding vane
The sliding vane supercharger uses a set of vanes mounted in an eccentric rotor. Although these are not very common in automotive performance applications, this is the type of pump that is used in air injection (air pump) emission control devices.

### Rotary piston
The rotary piston supercharger closely resembles a Wankel rotary engine like those found in the Mazda RX7. The rotor rotates through a series of three chambers to accelerate airflow.

## What the supercharger does
For most street applications, the job of a supercharger is much the same as the job of a turbocharger. When the throttle is wide open, it is desirable to fill each cylinder to 100 percent of its capacity. This means that each cylinder will contain air to the full atmospheric pressure of 14.7psi. If this is achieved it is said that the engine has 100 percent volumetric efficiency. Unfortunately the rather annoying path the air has to take on its journey prevents engines from achieving 100 percent volumetric efficiency. The engine driven supercharger is designed to compensate for this shortcoming in standard intake design.

Where the turbocharger depends primarily on the amount of heat energy in the exhaust, the supercharger's output is dependent on the speed of the engine. As a result the procedure of designing a supercharged power plant modification must begin by determining the desired level of boost. A typical street performance engine will run about 7 to 10lb of boost. This will typically be enough to achieve or even exceed 100 percent volumetric efficiency. Blower manufacturers offer very detailed information on matching their products to engines.

There are several advantages to the supercharger over the turbocharger. Of course, in the real world, every advantage will have a disadvantage. The primary advantage of the supercharger over the turbocharger is that the compressor is driven by the engine crankshaft. As a result the flow rate of the supercharger will always be proportional to engine rpm. The turbocharger will experience a lag while the flow and heat energy

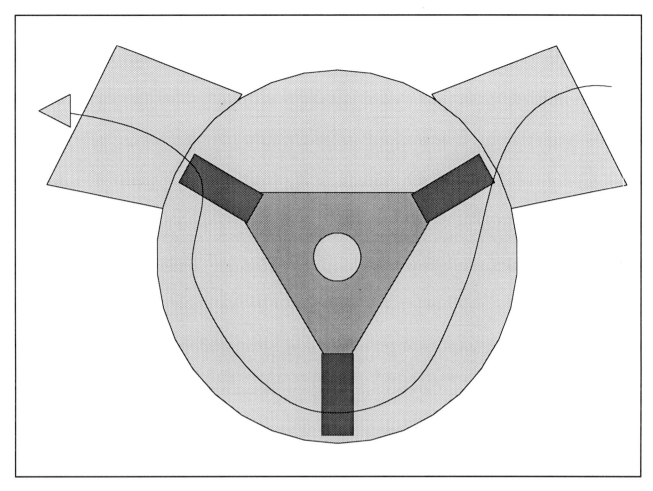

The sliding vane supercharger uses a set of vanes mounted in an eccentric rotor. Although these are not very common in automotive performance applications this is the type of pump that is used in air injection (air pump) emission control devices.

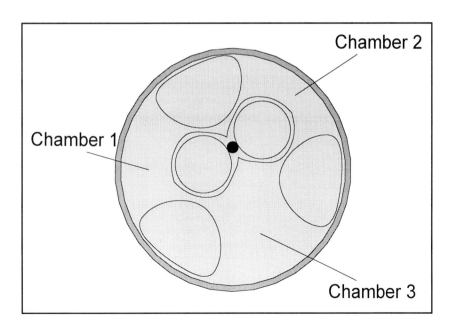

Chamber 2

Chamber 1

Chamber 3

of the exhaust gases overcomes the inertia of the turbine and compressor. The supercharger, being directly driven by the engine, does not suffer from lag. Therefore, even when the supercharger is not moving enough air to create boost, such as at low engine speeds, the supercharger is still helping to move air through the complicated twists and curves of the air induction system.

Left: The rotary piston supercharger is a lot like the Rootes supercharger except there is only one piston instead of two. This rotor rotates through a series of three chambers to accelerate air flow.

# Chapter 17

# Choosing the right Supercharger

If you are going to add a super-charger to an emission system equipped street vehicle, your choices become limited. The choices become even more limited when you live in California or any of the EPA designated non-attainment areas. In most areas, the only requirement for a legal installation is that all of the factory EPA certified emission control devices be retained and remain operative. Now that may seem easy, but in a typical super-charger installation the intake manifold is replaced with the su-percharger. This leaves no place for such devices as the EGR valve and air temperature sensors. Unless you are working on a pre-1966 model, the best way to select a supercharger is to by a California Air Resources Board approved kit.

The selection of the super-charger that is right for you be-gins with deciding how much boost you desire. Since the super-charger is driven by the engine, it is absolutely necessary that you decide exactly the rpm at which you desire this target boost. The supercharger would then have to be fitted with the correct crankshaft-to-blower drive ratio.

Let us begin. The chosen en-gine is a 350 Chevrolet. Now, se-lecting a desired boost is some-thing that should never be done by a man. I mean let's face it, a man is going to decide on several hundred pounds of boost... "I'm going to build an engine that will suck all the oxygen out of the planet's atmosphere." Realistical-ly, however, a little boost can go a long way. A street car with a 350 running 7lb of boost at 4500rpm will produce about 300horsepower. This is an im-provement of slightly less that 100 horsepower over the stock engine with a Quadrajet carbure-tor. Past 4500rpm, the stock en-gine horsepower output begins to drop off, the "blown" 350 will not peak until it reaches about 330hp at 5000rpm. This amounts to an improvement of 130hp. This fact nets a higher top speed for the vehicle.

## A 350 engine, 7lb of boost and a peak rpm of 5000 Pressure ratio

To calculate the pressure ratio we must first know estimat-ed airflow of the engine.

$$\frac{\text{Engine CID}}{1728} = \text{Cubic feet displacement}$$

$$\text{CFD} \times \frac{\text{Max RPM}}{2} = \text{ideal cfm}$$

$$\text{ieal cfm} \times 0.8 = \text{estimated actual cfm}$$

$$\frac{350}{1728} = 0.2025 \text{ Cubic feet displacement}$$

$$0.2025 \times \frac{5000}{2} = 506.25 \text{ cfm}$$

$$506.25 \times 0.8 = 405$$

$$\text{Presure ratio} = \frac{\text{Atmospheric Pressure Absolute} + \text{Boost}}{\text{Inlet Pressure Absolute}}$$

$$\text{Pressure ratio} = \frac{29.92 + (7 \times 2.03)}{29.92}$$

(Note: the above 2.03 converts PSI into inches of mercury.)

$$\text{Pressure ratio} = 1.47$$

## Legal Note
### 49 States

No installed device shall ren-der an emission control device in-operable. Any device installed on a 1968 or newer vehicle may not affect the installation or proper operation of any emission control device.

**Exceptions:**
• Any vehicle used exclusive-ly for racing purposes.
• Any newer engines used in pre-1968 vehicles.
• Marine applications.
• Stationary engines.

### California

No installed device shall ren-der an emission control device in-operable. Any device installed on a 1966 or newer vehicle may not affect the installation or proper operation of any emission control device. Additionally these devices must be a C.A.R.B. (California Air Resources Board) approved product with an issued E.O. (Ex-ecutive Order) number.

**Exceptions:**
• Any vehicle used exclusive-ly for racing purposes.
• and newer engines used in pre-1966 vehicles.
• Marine applications.
• Stationary engines.

| E.O. or Res. Number (Date) | Manufacturer "Product" (Model/Kit No.) | Vehicle Applications |
|---|---|---|
| D-150-1 (11/7/85) | K.F. Industries, Inc. "Max-25 Supercharger" | **85** and older Chevrolet/GMC light duty trucks & 86 and older AMC light duty trucks powered by GMC 2.8L V6 carbureted engine |
| D-150-2 (9/18/87) | K.F. Industries, Inc. "Max-25 Supercharger" | **86-88** Chevrolet/GMC light duty trucks powered by a GMC 2.8L V6 gasoline fuel injected engine |
| D-195-7 (10/1/91) | Paxton Products, Inc. "Supercharger Kit" Model SN-89, Part Nos. 1102000, 1103000, 1104000 | **86-92** Ford heavy duty trucks with a 460 CID multipoint gasoline fuel injected engine<br>**90-92** Ford and Mazda trucks with a multi point fuel injected engine |
| D-195-8 (10/1/91) | Paxton Products, Inc. "Supercharger Kit" Model SN-89, Part Nos. 10019, 10018, 2608789, 1101903, 1105000. 1213800, 1213900, 1214000 | **86-92** Ford trucks with 5.0L or 5.8L EFI engine<br>**86-92** Ford passenger cars with 5.0L EFI engine<br>**85-92** GM vehicles with 5.0L and 5.7L TPI/TBI engine<br>**88-92** GM trucks with 4.3L TBI engine<br>**88-92** GM trucks with 7.4 liter TBI engine<br>**88-92** BMW 735i with 3.4L EFI engine<br>**89-92** BMW 535I with 3.4L EFI engine<br>**88-89** BMW 635csi with 3.4L EFI engine |
| D-213-3 (2/20/92) | Vortech Engineering, Inc. "Model V-1 Supercharger" | **86-92** Ford passenger cars with 302 (5.0L) EFI engine |
| D-213-4 (2/20/92) | Vortech Engineering, Inc. "Model V-1 460 CID Supercharger" | **87-92** Ford passenger cars with 460 (7.5L) EFI engine |

Above and Right: Blowers are a way of saying raw power to the opposition. Many new vehicle applications are beginning to improve their performance with superchargers. Several manufacturers produce street legal superchargers for a wide range of aftermarket installations.

# Index